1
THING
MOMMA
DIDN'T
TELL US!
YOU LIVE, LOVE, & LEARN.
K. J'heneil

1 Thing Momma Didn't Tell Us! *YOU LIVE, LOVE & LEARN.*

Copyright© 2023 by K. J'heneil

Book design: Picturesque Designs, Media & Promos

This book is intended solely for your enjoyment and enlightenment.
Mature audiences only (18+).

ISBN: 979-8-3764-5897-6

In Loving Memory of
R.L.S

Create your unique username:

CHAPTER 2: BODY

CHAPTER 3: SOUL

Maybe if Momma had been candid about how difficult life can be, we would have been better prepared to deal with the inevitable ups and downs in our personal and professional lives. On the other hand, there may have been times when we flat-out refused to pay attention.

This is not a criticism, since our predecessors freely admitted that they, too, gained knowledge and experience as time went on. Let's face it: many were reared in religious households where important topics were off-limits, and some of those taboos persist today.

Thankfully, learning is possible at any age, so we must ensure that the next generation knows what life is like for a woman in the twenty-first century; and the fact that members of the millennial generation are not hesitant to confront challenges head-on is an encouraging sign.

After months of planning, researching, and writing, I am happy to provide you with this essential lifestyle book and personal diary. Even though puberty typically begins around the age of 14-17, this book is best for readers who are 18 and older.

We'll address a few controversial topics that have come up time and time again, as well as in the realm of social media. Aspects of interpersonal connections, with family, friendships, relationships, self-awareness, sex, and intimacy, will be explored.

The problems and challenges that arise in modern interpersonal relationships are complex, and many have their roots in destructive habits that have been passed down over the years. This book is a great investment since you will be able to add your own insights, perspectives, and stories to those already included. There are times when we are too caught up in the here and now to reflect on our past and present. Even if some of the issues covered may be challenging to digest, keeping a private diary serves as a form of self-therapy and offers a protected environment in which to share thoughts and experiences, both of which can contribute to the process of healing and taking responsibility for one's own actions.

The importance of this book to young women will grow as they progress through life, so persuade those you care about to get a copy. I sincerely hope you learn something here that you didn't know before and that it helps you out in some way. Take what is meant for you, and as the wise old proverb goes, "If it doesn't apply, let it fly. "

Mind

CHAPTER 1

THEN AND NOW!

Quote:

"There is nothing permanent except change." — Heraclitus.

The '80s and '90s gave us neon fashion, cassette tapes, and family barbecues where everyone brought way too much potato salad. But fast forward to today, and while TikTok dances and DoorDash might dominate, some things never change—like the importance of a tight-knit family when life gets real. It's wild to think how much has evolved, but what always remains is that feeling of belonging and the value of those who have your back.

We were incredibly inventive as kids, creating new and engaging games with whatever we had on hand -some were imaginary. Never complaining, just making the most of it, as every object in our collection was sentimental to us, no matter how much or how little it was worth.

Like many other girls at the time, I wrote daily diaries, and I can recall how much I treasured and looked forward to playing with my large doll collection that spanned my childhood and adolescence. I subsequently discovered that dolls are praised for their psychological, educational, and interpersonal benefits.

DID YOU PLAY WITH DOLLS AS A CHILD?   YES OR NO

WHAT PERCENTAGE OF YOUNG GIRLS
AGES 10-14 DO YOU THINK STILL PLAY
WITH DOLLS?   ________ %

We can all agree that one of the most challenging aspects of adolescence was the lack of privacy, and the most difficult component for parents was whether or not to invade and when they did, dealing with the shock of what they learned. Maybe this is one of the reasons why items such as dairies are not as popular as they once were, and most things are now kept hidden behind passwords on electronic devices.

As a child, I was happy for the presence of diaries since they provided an easy way to record my ideas and feelings. There weren't many other options available back then. Journals, like personal planners for women today, provided me with a creative outlet during my adolescence. They act as personal assistants for me, tracking my annual goals and sending reminders when needed. Journals are a great way to reflect on your life and make plans for the future. I believe that everyone should have one.

DID YOU KEEP A PERSONAL DIARY WHEN YOU WERE YOUNGER? 

WAS IT BENEFICIAL DURING YOUR TEENAGE YEARS? 

EXPLAIN WHY

FAMILY TIME

Back then quality time and sleepovers were at Grandma's house, where everyone gathered, and the delicious aromas emanating from baked goods and well-prepared food filled the air. It's always amazing how food can bring people together in both joyful and difficult times. When it came to holidays and other special events, a meal prepared at home was naturally favored over some fast-food restaurant. On Sundays was no different, many families, including ours, attended church, followed by a delicious home-cooked meal, evening drives, and sweet treats.

Vacations by far have been some of the best experiences I've had with my family, despite the fact that we frequently had to rush or be patient because someone had overslept, wasn't ready, or complained about lengthy commutes. The large vehicles, matching clothes, and theme parks are surely some unforgettable times.

We may all agree that strong familial ties have been found to have a significant impact on children's development, which may not have been everyone's experience, but it has been demonstrated that this plays a positive role. Structure in children's lives benefits them greatly because it gives them something to emulate and pass down to future generations.

HOW OFTEN, IF AT ALL, COULD YOU ATTEND SLUMBER PARTIES AS A CHILD?

☐ OFTEN   ☐ OCCASIONALLY   ☐ NOT AT ALL

PICTURES 'PICS'

Momma often forgets that when we were adolescents, we didn't spend our time snapping selfies daily, but we did hang out with our peers at the mall photo booths on weekends or at local photography studios. We would get dressed up in what we considered our best attire, as we eagerly awaited the development of our photographs, which could take minutes, hours, or days.

While it's understandable that parents may be baffled or at times annoyed by their children's incessant need to document every waking moment with a photograph, it's also clear that photography is still an integral part of modern life, both because it provides a record of events and because it serves as a wonderful reminder of the era in which those events took place. The expression *"memories don't leave like people do"* is exactly why I enthusiastically embrace opportunities to record priceless experiences.

EVOLUTION

It's fascinating to see how some historical figures and cultural moments have become less significant over time. The widespread use of various forms of technology that have significantly improved throughout civilization has, for the most part, served to build barriers in the way of human interaction with one another. As a member of the millennial generation, I was able to observe this merger firsthand, children of today have no idea what it was like to be a child in our day. Similarly, to this, our entire understanding of our parents' formative years is reliant on their memories, which, depending on how you view them, can be fascinating and puzzling.

We all yearn for the "good old days," but expecting things to stay the same given that we all come from different eras is both unrealistic and nonsensical.

NEW AGE PARENTING

It's easy to assume that today's parents feel the need to prove something to themselves, their kids, and the world at large. In reality, the vast majority of parents make decisions based on a sincere desire to provide their offspring with a far better upbringing than they had, regardless of the outcome. Given that children are so advanced, they are much more receptive for a shorter amount of time, and it is during this time that we are obligated to instill in them the knowledge and perspectives that will serve them well for the rest of their lives.

We understand that finding a balance between indulging our children and imposing strict rules can be challenging. Raising children in the modern era is both costly and demanding. Although we cannot turn back time, we can instill in the younger generation an appreciation for the timeless values and innovations that make life today so captivating and enjoyable.

IN A FEW WORDS, DESCRIBE YOUR DEFINITION OF 'GOOD PARENTING':

HOW WAS YOUR CHILDHOOD? (AGES 3-6)

1 **2** **3** **4** **5**

HORRIBLE   AVERAGE   AMAZING

HOW WAS YOUR CHILDHOOD? (AGES 7-10)

1 **2** **3** **4** **5**

HORRIBLE   AVERAGE   AMAZING

HOW WAS YOUR ADOLESCENCE? (AGES 11-14)

1 **2** **3** **4** **5**

HORRIBLE   AVERAGE   AMAZING

HOW WAS YOUR TEENAGE YEARS? (AGES 15-18)

1 **2** **3** **4** **5**

HORRIBLE   AVERAGE   AMAZING

SUMMARIZE YOUR CHILDHOOD STORY:

The children of a nation are often considered to be that nation's best hope for the future.

WHAT ARE SOME WAYS IN WHICH THE GOALS YOU HAVE FOR RAISING YOUR CHILDREN MAY DIFFER FROM THE WAY YOU WERE BROUGHT UP?

THE WORLD OWES US NOTHING!

Quote:

*"Don't go around saying the world owes you a living.
The world owes you nothing. It was here first." - Mark Twain*

REFLECTION

I came to this conclusion in my late teenage years: if I wanted to be successful and independent, I would have to make plans and arrange my life in the most effective way possible. I also put in a lot of work, which included long overtime, and tried to make decisions that would help me get closer to my long-term goals. What interested me, I carefully dissected, and what didn't, I left in place.

Now that I'm an adult and can look back on my own life and the lives of others, I've realized that we often make things more difficult for ourselves than they need to be, in our daily lives.

Have you noticed that we almost always invite trouble into our lives when we start putting our faith in other people and entrusting them to make important decisions for us? It is unfortunate that to be successful in different aspects of life, we may have to sacrifice some of our freedom in exchange for the love, respect, or mutual trust of others. This is a reality of life that we must accept.

Trusting people we don't know, our partners, colleagues, and even family members, is an essential part of life, and we must learn from our experiences whether good or bad.

Many people have had to learn this lesson the hard way after pouring their hearts and souls into careers, initiatives, or relationships that ultimately fail. The best thing we can do for ourselves is heed red flags, never dismiss our intuition, and make the changes that are needed quickly. In some cases, this may mean starting over. I agree that this is never a pleasurable feeling, especially since the time that was wasted cannot ever be regained. However, we must always do what is necessary for the betterment of ourselves.

SEQUENCE

Through years of observing human nature, I have committed myself to always try to have the final say in decisions that would have a lasting impact on my life or that I would need to live with. To be successful in life, it is important to maintain a positive attitude and remain focused on your passions, ideals and promises to yourself. While I understand that there is always room for growth, recognizing situations where things could have gone differently if I had not trusted my instincts has given me confidence in my ability to make wise decisions. One of my strengths is my ability to view a situation from multiple perspectives and then logically argue why the conclusion I have chosen will benefit me the most. This practice involves observing and learning from patterns and principles.

I recommend taking some time alone to carefully explore all of your alternatives so that your next big step is something you can commit to and feel good about. Nobody can give you better advice than you can, although advice from reputable sources may be beneficial, keep in mind that you are the one who must live with the outcomes of your choices.

MICROWAVE SOCIETY

You may come across people of all ages who believe that they can achieve their desired outcome by simply snapping their fingers. They may be willing to trample on others to get what they want faster, and won't care if it damages their reputation or how others feel. Despite this, these advocates of the *"I deserve it"* mentality often feel that they have the right to a better-than-average life, including a high standard of living and a variety of material comforts. This mentality can lead to activities such as losing their ability to think logically and resorting to extreme tactics to attain their goals. Individuals with an inflated sense of self-importance tend to think that the world owes them something for their relatively little contributions to society, or possibly nothing at all.

It's common for people to use titles and awards to justify their position, especially when comparing themselves to others in terms of social status. Unfortunately, this behavior is often seen in older generations and has been passed down to younger ones, which may influence their attitudes towards success and entitlement. This cycle creates an unfair and unbalanced society where deserving individuals are often overlooked. It's important to be aware of your surroundings and the actions of those around you to avoid getting caught up in negative patterns and traits as you go through life.

ACCOUNTABILITY

It can sometimes feel like people don't fully understand the link between hard work and success, and there is a general lack of optimism when faced with challenges. The phrase "Everyone has the same 24 hours in a day" has been said many times before, but it's how you spend your time that sets you apart from those who have success stories to tell.

For instance, if you wake up at 5 a.m. and start your day, compared to someone who wakes up at 8 a.m., there is a significant time difference that results in fewer opportunities for you to achieve your daily goals. We should take advantage of every opportunity available to us, as we are capable of doing so.

STRONG BACK

When we think about those who came before us, we realize that they put in a lot of work to create the opportunities that are available to us today. Even though we now live in a different era than that of our ancestors, we must never lose sight of the significant contributions they made or the burdens they bore to pave the way for us. They fought a hard battle, so we shouldn't expect everything to be easy.

Regardless of how many modern conveniences we have at our disposal, the things that must be done to be successful have not changed. If we follow in their footsteps and put into practice the wisdom that they passed on to us, we may find solace in their achievements and know that our hard work and determination will eventually pay off in the end.

As parents, we all want our children to have a better start than we did. To accomplish this, we must work hard, earn money, save it, and invest properly. The world is continually changing, and the expectations for success are rising. So we must adapt and educate our children that success involves hard effort, perseverance, and remaining loyal to oneself.

It is important to keep in mind that obtaining success through immoral means can have major implications, including embarrassment, mental anguish, and, in many cases, criminal liability. Honesty and integrity are critical components of success, but maintaining them requires effort and commitment. We must accept responsibility for our choices and endeavor to create the life and world we desire. Let us stop blaming others and start working towards a better future.

ARE YOU MAKING PROGRESS TOWARD YOUR GOALS IN LIFE?

DO YOU THINK IT'S EVER OK TO STEP ON SOMEONE'S TOES TO GET AHEAD?

HAVE YOU INHERITED ANYTHING THAT CAN GIVE YOU A HEAD START IN LIFE?

DO YOU INTEND TO LEAVE INHERITANCE FOR YOUR CHILDREN?

DO YOU BELIEVE PARENTS ARE OBLIGATED TO PAY FOR THEIR CHILDREN'S COLLEGE EDUCATION?

Notes!

EIGHTY20 TWIST

Quote:
Never give up 80% for 20%.

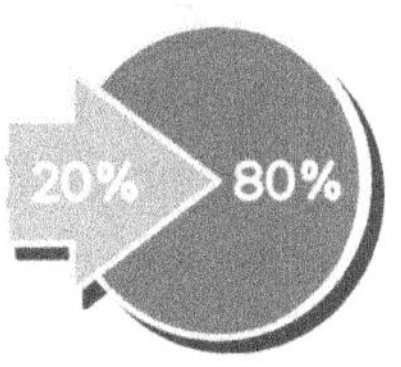

SYMPTOMS

The 80/20 rule, also known as the Pareto Principle, is a valuable guideline to consider when addressing problems or challenges. To develop effective solutions, it's important to thoroughly examine the situation from multiple perspectives and identify the underlying causes. Often, problems arise from neglect or improper treatment, which can lead to long-term negative effects in both personal and professional contexts. Therefore, it is crucial to approach each situation mindfully, as dismissing or overlooking issues can exacerbate the problem.

This principle can be applied to both positive and negative experiences, helping to make sense of various outcomes. An alternate interpretation of the 80/20 rule is that 20% of your efforts or concerns can significantly impact the remaining 80% of your results. This aspect of the rule is particularly useful in a business environment, where it enables individuals and teams to prioritize their tasks effectively and focus on what is most important.

By concentrating on the vital 20% of actions that contribute to success, you can achieve significant improvements in your outcomes.

Amazingly, even if you devote only 20% of your time and energy to a project or activity, you can increase your chances of success by up to 80%. This knowledge enables individuals and organizations to work smarter, not harder, ensuring that efforts are matched with meaningful outcomes.

Always prioritize tasks and track your thoughts to decide the best next steps, while taking time to evaluate your situation and avoid feeling overwhelmed. The fact is time passes regardless, so aim to be early for meetings, interviews, or work to prevent serious consequences. Balancing personal and professional life is key to success. Building strong relationships, whether with a partner, friends, or colleagues, requires time and effort, so invest wisely in these areas.

You will find that the 80/20 rule is a valuable tool for improving performance, prioritizing tasks, and solving problems more effectively.

You may want to consider the following questions:
Where do your priorities lie?

☐ WORK   ☐ FRIENDS

☐ LOVE INTEREST   ☐ HOBBIES (GYM, BAR, SPORTS)

☐ SCHOOL   ☐ CLUBS & ORGANIZATIONS

☐ CHILDREN   ☐ RELATIONSHIP

☐ SOCIAL MEDIA   ☐ OTHER: _______________

☐ CHURCH

____

On average, what percentage <u>each week</u> do you have meaningful interactions with:

Family __________ % Friends __________ % Partner __________ %

Can you remember a time in your romantic relationship when you felt as if something was missing?

Every day, people experience a wide range of emotions, but one of the most challenging aspects is managing the consequences of our actions. In committed relationships, the effects of emotions are often short-lived and superficial. Unfortunately, many individuals abandon their marriages and families—often the most significant parts of their lives—for fleeting, temporary pleasure. This weakness in human nature plays a major role in why so many people, despite vows and promises, may secretly desire to leave their partners for a single lifestyle.

The constant craving for more is a major source of both dissatisfaction and reckless behavior. Such thinking should be avoided, as most people don't fully realize the implications of their choices until it's too late, often leading to regret and guilt. Although life may appear better on the other side, a person's behavior often reveals deeper truths. For instance, it is highly unlikely that a perfect "Prince Charming" would be pursuing someone already in a committed relationship.

Some men, unfortunately, are skilled at concealing their true relationship status, even when they have a family or significant other who remains unaware of their actions. This can become a trap for many women, leading them to invest emotionally without realizing the full extent of the situation. Once deeply involved, it becomes harder to think rationally and make clear decisions.

These men often present themselves as seeking casual relationships or just looking for fun, rather than committing to something serious. People tend to hide their flaws and showcase their best selves when pursuing someone. It's important not to sacrifice the steady 80% of happiness you have, even if it feels routine or dull at times, for a fleeting 20% that might bring temporary excitement but could ultimately lead to regret and sorrow.

Moving Forward

If you find yourself tempted to explore such a situation, take a step back and carefully consider the potential consequences. Weigh the positive and negative impacts, not just on yourself but on your partner and others connected to your lives. Sometimes, people give up on relationships too soon, missing the chance to let them flourish. It's easy to walk away and seek something new, but meaningful connections take effort.

Especially if you have children, staying committed to working on your relationship requires even more courage, resilience, and patience. Seeking therapy or talking to someone who has experienced a similar situation can be incredibly helpful, even if some may disagree with this approach. Above all, open and honest communication with your partner is often the most effective way to address challenges and move forward together.

HOW MANY RELATIONSHIPS HAVE <u>YOU</u> ABANDONED TOO SOON?

HOW MANY EXES DID YOU FEEL, BROKE UP WITH YOU FOR NO VALID REASON?

HAVE YOU EVER RUINED A WONDERFUL SITUATION BY BEHAVING INAPPROPRIATELY DUE TO YOUR EMOTIONS?

YES OR NO

SHARE YOUR MOST MEMORABLE 80/20 SITUATION:

WHAT DID SITUATIONS TEACH YOU?

GIVE THE WORLD NOTHING YOU MAY WANT TO TAKE BACK!

Quote:

"Avoid popularity if you would have peace." - Abraham Lincoln

The majority of our waking hours are spent in front of a screen, either actively participating in some form of social interaction or idly monitoring the activities of others. This could be done for a variety of reasons. The "now" society that we live in encourages us to share everything about ourselves, from the food that we eat to the thoughts and feelings that go through our minds at any given moment.

Today's parents were caught off guard when they learned that technology in all of its guises would prove to be both a boon and a bane and that it would even prove to be their most formidable adversary when it came to the task of raising their children. Nevertheless, here we are!

The time spent on social media is not only rewarding in and of itself but also beneficial to the pursuit of professional and personal goals. We can all agree on this since, despite the pandemic, most of us were still able to keep in touch with one another and learn about worldwide developments. Despite its many advantages, social media can have positive as well as adverse effects.

SOCIAL MEDIA LIFE IS REAL LIFE

It is each individual's responsibility to hold themselves accountable for their moral and ethical behavior. Those in particular professions and positions of public trust, on the other hand, are expected to demonstrate an even greater level of morality and ethics in their daily lives. People in positions of power, like teachers, lawmakers, clergy, and elected officials, are continually evaluated and tested for their behavior. As a result, people should behave and communicate consistently, whether in person or online. Those occupations are more than simply a job; they are a way of life, and anyone who does not believe they can handle the stress and high standards involved may want to look elsewhere for employment.

PROACTIVE

Even though we may be communicating with someone who is on the other side of the world, we still feel the pressure to come out as the winner in online conversations. Unfortunately, we often end up getting into intense confrontations, losing our cool, and verbally attacking each other. It is best to avoid engaging in such behaviors unless you enjoy wasting your time and energy.

The internet's anonymity encourages people to express their critical thoughts more daringly than they would in person. Being harassed online can disrupt someone's entire day or even their entire existence. While most of us have had thoughts of revenge at some point in our lives, we have now grown to realize that acting on those impulses would be a waste of precious time and energy that could be used for more productive activities.

Not everyone can remain neutral during a conversation, but it's essential to do so. As a wise man once said, "You should never argue with someone who has nothing to lose". This advice applies both online and offline and should be kept in mind at all times.

Taking care of your mental health is essential, no matter your feelings of pride or embarrassment. Even if it seems like you have lost the argument and the other side has won, it's crucial to protect your mental well-being.

Before posting, commenting, or responding to anything, consider how your words might impact the situation. When both sides have valid reasons regarding an issue, it's best to agree to disagree. Remember that maintaining civility and respect for others is always the right thing to do.

ADD | FOLLOW | SUBSCRIBE

It's a great honor for us when someone invites us to join their social media network, whether you believe this theory or not. People usually follow someone's life out of genuine interest or curiosity. However, accepting a request means giving access to a wide range of personal and private information, as well as social interactions. This can make your good or bad opinions and life public and open to scrutiny. Sadly, for many people, this is where they face their initial concerns and troubles with social media sites.

BOUNDARIES

It's important to be aware of people who are excessively critical, demanding, or use their acquaintance with you for personal gain. Negative individuals can come from unexpected places, even from those you care about the most. If someone or something is making you unhappy, decreasing your self-esteem, or jeopardizing your personal space, it's best to get rid of them.

Remember, you have the power to decide how to respond to any given situation and can take your time to do so. Don't let others have too much control over your life. Instead of airing your problems online, try having a private conversation with the person directly involved if things worsen. You will eventually learn to recognize that not all calls for your attention are necessary, and it's much more important to select fights with beneficial outcomes.

PRIVACY

It's important to remember that a forwarded message or screenshot can quickly become a source of conflict if it's shared in a context where it was not intended to be discussed. Therefore, it's wise to avoid posting anything online that you wouldn't want the entire world to see. Unfortunately, some individuals are naturally inclined towards mischief, and idleness, and have a lot of free time, regardless of their occupation.

When participating in a global community on the internet, it's crucial to respect the social media habits of others. It's also best to avoid engaging with individuals who constantly bring up other people in conversation, especially if it's in a negative light. Do you believe that the world would be a better place if everyone adopted this mentality? (YES) OR (NO)

WHO ARE THE FOUR MOST TOXIC PEOPLE IN YOUR SOCIAL CIRCLE?

[A] HAVE YOU EVER MET SOMEONE WHO ACTS DRASTICALLY DIFFERENT ONLINE, THAN IN PERSON?

YES OR NO

I. HOW MUCH DOES [A] MATTER TO YOU? STATE YOUR REASONS.

1　　**2**　　**3**　　**4**　　**5**

NOT
IMPORTANT

VERY
IMPORTANT

WHAT ARE THE REASONS YOU ACCEPT FRIEND REQUESTS FROM SOMEONE YOU DON'T KNOW ON SOCIAL MEDIA?

1 ____

____

____

2 ____

____

____

3 ____

____

____

DO YOU POST/TAG YOUR CURRENT LOCATION?   YES OR NO

DO YOU MERGE YOUR WORK/BUSINESS WITH YOUR PERSONAL SOCIAL MEDIA LIFE?   YES OR NO

[A] DO YOU GET INVOLVED IN ONLINE CONFLICTS?   YES OR NO

[B] HOW OFTEN? ______________________

WHICH ONES ARE YOU MOST PASSIONATE ABOUT ONLINE? ✓

- ○ General News
- ○ Politics
- ○ Controversy
- ○ Social Injustices
- ○ Relationships

- ○ Health & Body
- ○ Celebrity News
- ○ Gossip
- ○ Everything
- ○ Other

____

(C) HOW MANY HOURS PER DAY DO YOU SPEND ONLINE?

_____________ / 24-HOURS

WHAT POSITIVE ACTIVITIES DO YOU ENGAGE IN WHEN YOU'RE NOT USING SOCIAL MEDIA? (IN ADDITION TO EMPLOYMENT AND STUDIES)

(1) _______________________________________

(2) _______________________________________

(3) _______________________________________

(4) _______________________________________

ENERGY SAVING TIPS

- Don't post social media content you may not want other people's opinions or comments on.

- Don't succumb to anger and conflict and then air your 'dirty laundry' on the Internet.

- Don't post or share anything explicit on the Internet that you might later regret.

- It is important to refrain from sharing personal information such as your current address or location in public forums for your safety.

- Don't isolate your social life from your everyday existence. Be genuine!

- Don't discuss any personal information that could potentially cause embarrassment to yourself or others in the future, including family, friends, and children.

- Don't compromise your job by sharing personal, sensitive, or unauthorized data/pictures.

- Do be considerate and respectful of other people's feelings and privacy.

- Do balance your online and offline time daily.

- Do your research before conducting business or meeting strangers online.

A SIMPLE GOLDEN RULE IS TO TREAT OTHERS THE WAY YOU WOULD LIKE TO BE TREATED.

HINT! HINT!

Always read the room...

As you grow older, you will notice that people around you have unique personalities, behaviors, and habits. By observing someone's body language and facial expressions, you can gain insights into their mental and emotional state. It's also important to pay attention to how others respond to your questions and concerns.

It's possible to gain knowledge about someone by analyzing their attributes, even if you've never met them in person. A person's preferences, vocabulary, and emotions can offer important insights into their personality. These insights can help you grow as a person and establish healthy boundaries in your relationships. Although we may have received guidance in our childhood, we must ensure that we continue on the path of self-improvement.

The art of reading between the lines:

Visiting
- Pay attention to others' body language and nonverbal cues, so you don't overstay your welcome.
- Unexpectedly showing up at someone's home or workplace can be perceived as impolite and intrusive.

Conversing
- Do not overstep boundaries or invade someone's privacy if you haven't been invited.
- Be aware of when to end a conversation and when to start.

- If someone avoids discussing a recent incident by changing the subject, likely, they are not yet ready to talk about it.
- When someone crosses their arms, it is a global symbol of boredom, and it is unlikely that they are interested in what you are saying.
- When someone rests their hands on their laps or at their sides, they are probably feeling comfortable and content.
- A person's level of impatience can be gauged by the extent to which their hands are resting on their hips.

Arguing

- Make your point, and then move on. Recognizing that everyone has different perspectives.
- When someone leaves the scene of a conflict, what they say may indicate their desire for revenge.

Cellphone

- If someone frequently ignores your calls or delays replying to your messages, it is likely because they are busy, distracted, or uninterested in engaging.
- Some individuals are reluctant to participate in impromptu video conversations because they feel it may come across as presumptuous.
- If a person flips their phone over or turns off the ringer, it could suggest that they are trying to hide something from those around them. This behavior may seem harmless, but it can often be incriminating. It could also be a habit from the past.

Can you read body language well? (YES) OR (NO)

Did you ever share a living space with a friend? (YES) OR (NO)

a. Have your experiences been successful? (YES) OR (NO)

"Would you ask a visitor to leave if they stayed at your home longer than you expected?" (YES) OR (NO)

How do you handle unexpected guests?

We all may feel that our opinion is right, do you truly value the opinions of others? (YES) OR (NO)

What are the signals that someone wants you to leave?

LOOKS, LIKES & LOVES!

Seek respect, not attention. It lasts longer. – Ziad K. Abdelnour

THE BAD

In today's world, it has become a habit to look for interesting videos or articles to share on social media. People enjoy it, as it makes their days go by quickly and helps them deal with difficult situations. Whether it's trending topics, funny content, sad stories, or drama, we love it all. For some individuals, sharing content on social media is a way to earn a living and support themselves or their families. All they need is a large audience that engages with their posts by commenting, interacting, and sharing their work.

It's not exactly rocket science, as most successful content creators believe that people should act in ways that attract attention, whether for personal pleasure or for financial gain. Consequently, they don't appear to care about what they post or share online, even if it means hurting someone's feelings. Others have a natural desire to compare their own lives with those of others, particularly celebrities, to improve themselves and feel better about their situation.

As online communities are built on mutual interaction, we want others to value our social media relationships just as much as we do theirs. Unfortunately, this desire for validation and approval can lead to a dark side of social media that is disguised as love and likes.

It's always surprising to me when I hear people say they don't have time for social media. Research shows that those who have mentally and physically demanding jobs spend less time on social media than the average person. However, people from all over the world are constantly connected online, regardless of their location. Some individuals are so engrossed and distracted by social media attention that they are unable to disconnect from their devices.

Many businesses have reported lower worker productivity as a result of social media usage and have even blocked access to social media and other websites. Scientists have found that receiving "likes" on social media activates the brain's reward system, which can lead to an imbalance that may negatively affect both personal and professional lives.

SOCIAL KIDS

Today's children are more technologically advanced than ever before. They enjoy experimenting with new dances, stunts, and other activities to gauge their classmates' reactions. However, what happens if they don't receive any positive feedback?

Children learn by observing and imitating, much like little sponges. Due to their developing brains, children are susceptible to confusion, distraction, and exposure. Therefore, using them as attention-getters, stickers, or content might not be a good idea.

Young children depend on their parents to guide them and make decisions that are beneficial for them until they are old enough to make their own choices. It is difficult to correct past mistakes or delete irrelevant comments from the internet.

LEVELS

One thing that you might have observed is that people participate in a wide range of attention-seeking behaviors, which can range from moderate to severe. Some examples of these behaviors include the following:

1. Using one's successes as bait to attract positive attention. LIKES/LOVES.

2. Using controversy to get people riled up, ANGRY, SHOCKED,

3. Using people or situations to gain popularity or credibility.

4. Willing to do anything to get guidance, help, or MORE viewers.

5. Telling lies or making up details to get people to, sympathize, or send funds.

6. Posting nudity or sexy images/videos.

STATE OF MIND

People who constantly say or do things to bring attention to themselves may cause significant disturbance in their social circles. Some people may go to considerable lengths to avoid these behaviors at any cost.

Two *points to consider:*
1. What lengths are individuals willing to go to to improve their self-esteem, social position, and reputation among their peers?
2. When does a person's desire for attention go beyond being annoying and into the territory where it's necessary to confront them or seek mental help?

Have you ever gone to extreme levels to impress your social media friends & followers?

Explain the importance of doing so if you answered "yes" to the previous question.

How important is it for you to get feedback from friends and followers after you hit "publish" or "send" on a post, or even after you comment?

1 **2** **3** **4** **5**

NOT
IMPORTANT

VERY
IMPORTANT

Do you react to your own post(s)?
Why?

YES OR NO

Do you find yourself compelled to publish content that is either intriguing or designed specifically to get people's attention?

YES OR NO

Explain your answer.

What happens if individuals don't respond to your content in the way you anticipated?

HOW DO YOU FEEL?

____

____

WHAT DO YOU DO?

- ☐ REPOST
- ☐ MAKE A BETTER POST
- ☐ DELETE
- ☐ IT DOESN'T MATTER

What are your views on those individuals who constantly share or post information that is emotionally triggering or distasteful?

____

____

____

What are your usual reactions?

- ☐ SHARE IT.
- ☐ ASK THEM TO REFRAIN!
- ☐ IGNORE.
- ☐ MUTE/HIDE IT.
- ☐ REPORT IT.
- ☐ NOTHING.

THE GOOD

The use of social media can have both positive and negative impacts. It has been observed that social media is highly beneficial for businesses, both for marketing purposes and for impromptu engagement. Despite many CEOs not acknowledging it, Instagram posts, TikTok videos, and Facebook stories have helped companies receive advertising credits that would have otherwise cost them a significant amount of money, sometimes in the hundreds of thousands or even millions of dollars, for a single viral moment.

The emergence of young millionaires on websites like YouTube and other gaming platforms has made it possible for anyone to achieve a great life. With new innovative concepts entering the market every day, having a unique strategy is essential if you want to be part of the social media success stories. Instead of starting from scratch, it's easier to add your own spin on things. Everyone has a hidden skill that's waiting to be discovered.

What ideas do you have for improving the quality of your social media experience? Whether business or leisure time.

GOOD LOOKING AND WHAT?

Quote:

"Unique and different is the next generation of beautiful."

– Taylor Swift

Although it may sound like a cliché, it's important to remember that your physical appearance has nothing to do with your success in finding love or fulfilling societal expectations. However, the way you look can indeed affect how others approach and engage with you, especially in the dating scene. Sometimes, physical qualities can also play a role in opportunities such as jobs, gifts, rides, and promotions. For instance, many women spend a considerable amount of money to enhance their physical features like their buttocks, breasts, and waist, which shows that some features are more valued and sought after than others.

It's crucial to understand that while your appearance can reflect your mood and how your day has gone, it is not enough to maintain attention or build a relationship. Mental strength and emotional stability are also essential, and your mood can significantly impact how you interact with others.

STAGNATION

Let's take a moment to reflect on times when we were overly concerned with our appearance and missed out on fully enjoying the moment. This indicates the inner struggle we faced due to a lack of confidence and constant worries. Such tendencies prevented us from letting loose and indulging in activities as often as we should have.

Have you ever noticed that those who seem carefree and may be perceived by society as unattractive or unpopular are often the most enjoyable company?

Why do you think this is?

____

____

____

____

____

Do you think your appearance is your greatest asset?   

Has your lack of confidence ever prevented you from attending an extremely important event?  

Do others treat you differently because of how you look?  

Do you have good looks but were dumped by someone?   

Is there something about your appearance you wish you could alter? If so, why?

LOOSEN UP

If you're planning to go on a trip, it's important to have a good time and spend it with those who matter to you. Whether you're going camping, to a theme park, to the pool, or to another country, the most essential thing is to enjoy the experience.

Make sure to bring appropriate clothing and accessories, such as a swimsuit and a swim cap if you're going to a water park. Starting a trip or event with a negative attitude, like complaining about the weather or the quality of your accommodations, can ruin the experience for everyone involved. Inconsideration, tardiness, and disobedience to rules and others can also lead to trouble. It's important to remember that not every event requires the nicest attire, a five-star location, or a red-carpet entrance, focus on having fun and making memories instead. Wear comfortable clothes and shoes, like a baseball cap, sneakers, and a hair tie, so you can enjoy outdoor experiences to the fullest.

Living a meaningful life that brings you joy is what matters most. As social creatures, we crave novelty and excitement, and it's important to seek out new experiences to avoid becoming stagnant and boring personality.

Couples should spend time together doing shared activities at least twice a week. This can help maintain strong bonds and create lasting memories.

BEAUTY IS SUBJECTIVE

Do you frequently encounter men who are successful, intelligent, and physically appealing? 

If yes, how often?

What other factors stood out?

Have you ever noticed how some men can appear so distinct from one another while also sharing remarkable similarities? It's intriguing to think about.
You've probably encountered people who look to have it all - success, attractiveness, and a great personality - but after you get to know them, you realize they're not as amazing on the inside as they seem. These individuals may exhibit features like as boastfulness, overconfidence, and self-assurance, which can be seen as arrogance and make them difficult to be around.

It's important to remember that finding a decent companion isn't about your financial or social status. Respect, honesty, hard effort, and kindness are key values. Focusing on these characteristics enables you to attain success and happiness while avoiding shallow or excessive behavior.

You can reach your full potential if you are true to yourself and work hard, regardless of your appearance or upbringing. However, we may not be making the right dating choices. Maybe we're missing out on wonderful opportunities because we're not looking in the right places.

BAD vs GOOD KARMA

Can you imagine talking to someone who is not only physically attractive, but also has beautiful teeth and skin, is immaculately dressed, and exudes an intriguing aroma? However, after talking with them for five to ten minutes, you notice that their intelligence does not match their outer appearance. You should never wish to leave this impression on people.

As an adult, you are expected to engage in talks and contribute to group debates on a variety of issues, regardless of your intelligence or attractiveness.

Attending communication seminars, reading at least one book per month, and regularly practicing self-talk in front of a mirror are three of the most effective strategies to improve one's capacity to engage with others. You should also let go of unrealistic expectations, allow yourself to laugh at yourself now and then, and recognize that making errors and feeling ashamed is a natural part of the human experience.

A person with a short fuse and a tendency to lose their cool is likely to have a bad and unpleasant look in the majority of social situations. Your outer appearance alone will never determine your level of success in life as much as the charisma and genuineness with which you carry yourself.

"Would you be willing to ignore a person's negative attitude if they possess beauty and wealth?" 

Have you received any compliments from others indicating that they enjoy spending time with you? 

Are you easily offended? 

Are you a conversation starter? 

How fun are you at an outing?
1 - Playing cellphone games
2 - Chatting / Texting
3 - Observing
4 - Engaging others / Meeting new people
5 - Singing karaoke / Dancing / Tipsy

1 **2** **3** **4** **5**

You purchase a stunning gown for a party, but plans alter and you hear that it will include fun interactive activities, party food, and booze. Do you...

1 - Throw your own elegant party.
2 - Return the dress and stay home.
3 - Go, and have an amazing time.
4 - Keep the dress, choose something appropriate!
5 - Be upset/argue about the last-minute change.

1 **2** **3** **4** **5**

Which of the following would you most want to do to celebrate your birthday?

1 - Go to a fancy dinner.
2 - Watch a good movie.
3 - Do something thrilling, skydive!
4 - Take me Shopping!
5 - Watersport, snorkeling!
6 - Travel to another country!

1 **2** **3** **4** **5** **6**

"FOCUS ON YOURSELF!"

Quote:

"How you love yourself is how you teach others to love you."
—Rupi Kaur

It's common to hear the phrase "Focus on yourself", but many still struggle with it. Whether it's due to neglecting ourselves or constantly worrying about others, it's easy to lose sight of our own needs.

This often leads to a lack of introspection and self-care, which can contribute to the development of mental illnesses and the rise in suicides. To prevent this, we must prioritize our emotional well-being, regardless of who we are and where we are from. By taking the time to understand ourselves, our emotions, and our purpose in life, we can cultivate self-love and self-awareness.

Additionally, rushing into a relationship before understanding our own needs and desires can be a dangerous move. Remember, we all have a unique purpose in life, and discovering it is the first step in developing a healthy relationship with ourselves.

YOUNGER SELF

When young girls experience social discomfort, rejection, or confusion, they are at a higher risk of developing low self-esteem. Adolescence is the best time to develop a sense of self and personal values.

Self-esteem should be instilled in girls from a young age so that they are never reliant on a man to determine their worth.

Any adult can tell you that adolescence isn't always easy. A person's ability to see into the future could be impaired by physical changes and other pressures. During the naive and uncertain years of 18–25, many women make decisions that will impact the rest of their lives.

SELF AWARENESS

Have you ever wondered what it means to be a "total package"? It's a loaded question, and asking someone what they bring to the table can be a touchy subject. But you should feel confident in your answers to these questions. After all, you have unique talents and abilities that are valuable in their own right.

As parents, it's important to encourage our daughters to start building their own identities between the ages of 14 and 17. During these formative years, it's essential to avoid getting pregnant, settling down, or falling in love. Instead, focus on cultivating your strengths and interests. The world is at your fingertips, and you have the power to achieve anything you set your mind to. Whether you have a specific skill set or a broad range of knowledge, your strengths are what make you exceptional. By mastering a single talent, you'll set yourself up for success in any endeavor. The rewards of honing your abilities will come both materially and emotionally and will help you weather any challenges that come your way.

During the past lockdown, many people discovered hidden talents and started successful businesses from scratch. It's true what they say: you don't know how strong you are until you're pushed to your limits. But with a little introspection, you can discover your own unique set of skills and talents. Don't worry if you don't know what they are just yet. You, like everyone else, have something valuable to contribute to the world, keep seeking within.

LIFE HAPPENS

Having children can make it harder for individuals to focus on their finances and stick to healthy routines. Today's fast-paced world often leaves us feeling like there's never enough time or money to provide for our families. It can be surprising to see the questions and expectations that today's youth have, and how unforgiving they can be towards their circumstances. They are clever observers who hold grudges against decisions that impact them.

When planning for your future, don't settle for a life that's only slightly better than your upbringing. Instead, focus on bettering yourself. The first step towards overcoming negative behaviors and patterns is to become aware of them. For example, a young woman struggling to figure out her next steps could benefit from creating a vision board outlining her immediate goals. It's okay to try again if you don't get it right the first time. Sometimes, you may need to give up some of your favorite things to live the life you envision for yourself. Keep your mind on your objectives and the steps you need to take to achieve them. Remember that no one who has achieved greatness ever had it easy.

What is <u>the</u> biggest struggle you face?

What plans do you have to improve your existing situation?

List the generational curses and describe their effects on you and others:

1 ____

2

3

4

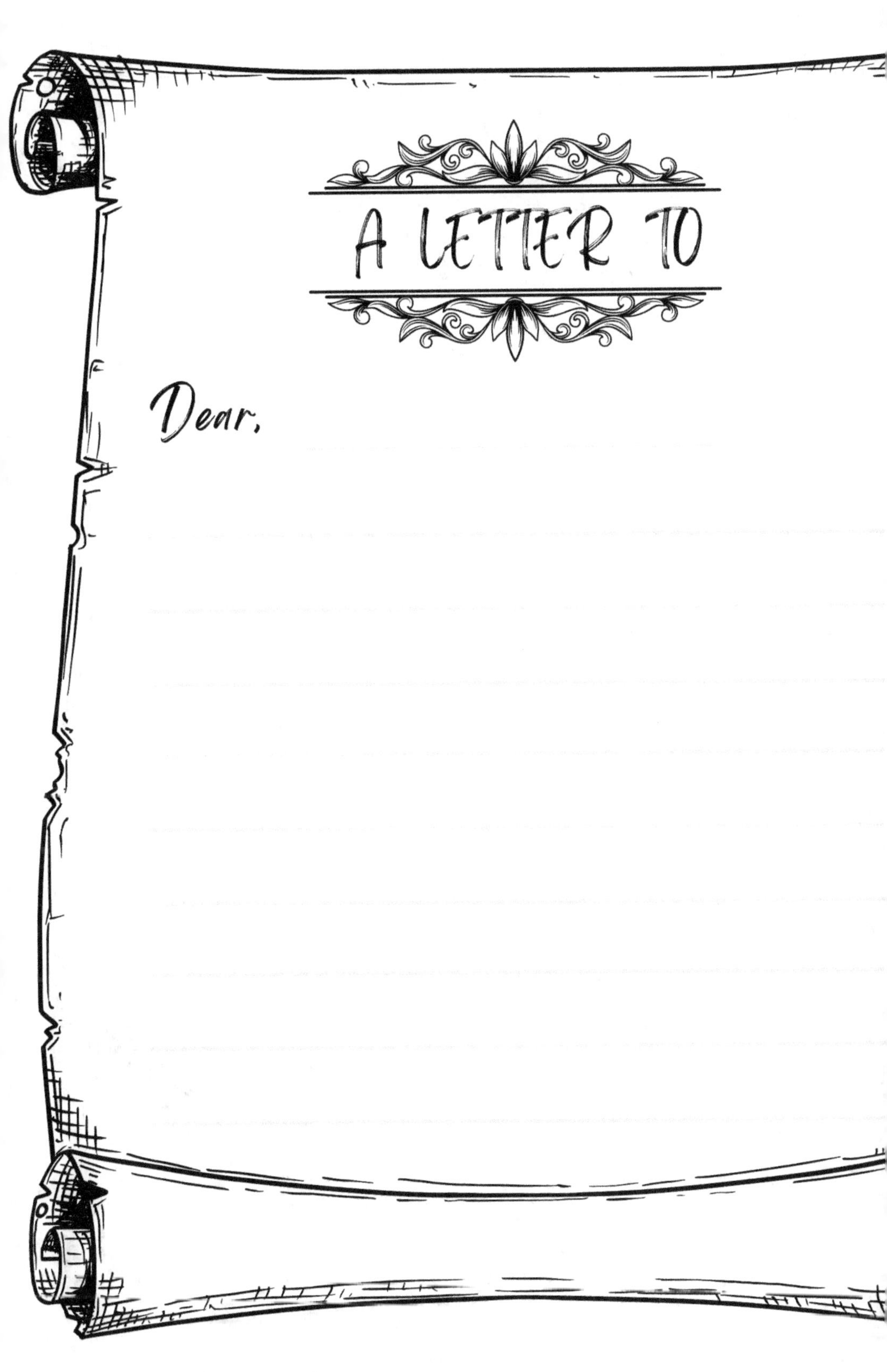

A LETTER TO
Dear,

YOURSELF
Sincerely,
Date:

KEEP YOUR HEART OFF YOUR SLEEVE!

Note:
Highly sensitive people may be more susceptible to being gaslighted.

REAL TALK

Being highly sensitive can feel like you're carrying a "Gaslight Me" sign on your forehead. But here's the flip side: that sensitivity? It's also your superpower.

In a world that's all about playing 4D chess with emotions, your awareness can protect you from being anyone's pawn. We've all seen the red flags—and ignored them, right? Not anymore. Tap into your self-confidence, own your emotional intelligence, and remember: not everyone deserves access to your inner world. Protect your peace, queen.

In contrast to men's ego, reason, and adrenaline, women navigate a complex, detail-oriented, and emotionally charged environment. If we had known this when we were younger, we could have saved ourselves a lot of pain and suffering. Yet, sometimes we don't give ourselves enough time to understand the whole picture. Nevertheless, we should keep living, loving, and learning.

There will be times in life when you may need to adopt a more assertive, masculine attitude, irrespective of whether you identify as a feminist or not. However, this does not undermine the significance of the "soft girl era." Rather, it gives us a fresh perspective on things and teaches us how to communicate effectively with people of the opposite gender.

On the other hand, it could be the solution to conquering challenges that require a lot of knowledge and self-confidence. Women are too perceptive to let themselves be manipulated as pawns in psychological games, especially when they are consistently exposed to negative manipulation and suffering.

SAFEKEEPING = SELF-LOVE

Pro Tip: Treat your secrets like your Netflix password —don't hand it out freely, especially not on a "free trial" basis. Think about it: when was the last time oversharing worked in your favor? Whether you're meeting someone new over brunch or vibing with someone on Bumble, some stories are better left untold until trust is earned. That drama about your last situationship or the tea about your bestie's betrayal? Yeah, that's not first-date material.

Here's why: not everyone you meet is as trustworthy as they seem, and some folks might use your openness against you. Think of your personal details as exclusive content—reserved only for the premium subscribers in your life. When in doubt, ask yourself: "Would I share this on a public Insta story?" If the answer is no, it's probably a no in person too.

Finally, remember that the outcome of a situation may not always be what you hoped for, but it's important to stay positive at all times, not be overly anxious, and always be prepared to move forward.

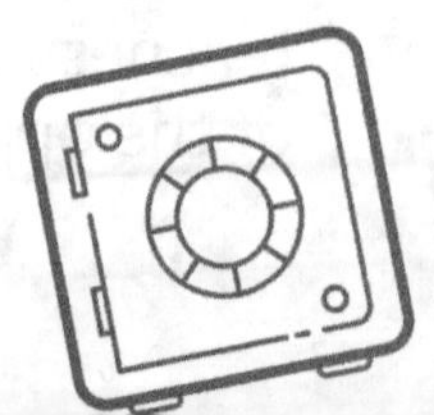

ELEMENT OF SURPRISE

If you try to live your life more systematically, you'll realize that there are many benefits to keeping certain things to yourself. It's not always a good idea to reveal your innermost thoughts and feelings, plans, secrets, upcoming period, or level of affection if it won't benefit you in any way. This doesn't mean that you should isolate yourself from society, but it does mean that you should carefully weigh the pros and cons of sharing your true identity.

One of the most admirable qualities in a man is his ability to stay composed in social situations and to read a woman's expressions and body language. For this and other reasons, men often pursue women in the beginning of a relationship, but in the end, it is the women who have to fight for their love.

On first dates, women are more likely to let their emotions guide their questions and responses instead of using logic or being direct. This can be awkward for both parties, but it's important to resist the urge to picture a future with someone after just one date. When looking for the man of your dreams, it's not logical or useful to jump to conclusions so soon.

People often act based on their beliefs about what's best for themselves, even if it's not necessarily accurate or the right thing to do. While we've been taught to believe that controlling our emotions is useful, it's important to strike a balance and not let our emotions control us completely.

Have you ever put your true feelings on display, and had those efforts pay off for you in the long run? 

Is there a reciprocation from the people you confided in about your innermost thoughts and feelings? 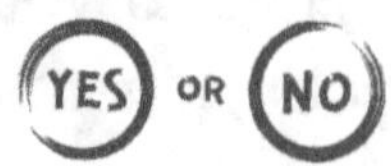

MANIPULATION

Numerous women have shared their experiences of being in situations where they felt unsafe and sought the help of trusted friends or family members. However, there are times when people abuse our trust and betray us by sharing our secrets with others, despite repeatedly promising to keep things confidential and showing respect for our privacy. This type of behavior is unfortunately common and can make it clear that it's better to keep certain personal details hidden to avoid being let down by those we trust.

As humans, we tend to criticize others, but why is that? Is it because we are wired to evaluate someone based on their habits or do we truly believe they deserve it? There could be numerous factors at play here, but one of the most significant ones is that people tend to classify and judge each other based on their social status and the level of respect they command. They use this information to target individuals who appear vulnerable. However, it's important to remember that our behavior, actions, and what we allow others to do to us determine how others treat us.

REALITY CHECK: GLOW UP STARTS WITHIN

Want to make your life more interesting? Start by aligning your vibe with your vision board—or better yet, your Instagram aesthetic. Seriously, your glow-up doesn't need a co-sign from anyone else.

Start small: pick a goal, like learning a new skill, improving your fitness, or curating a grid-worthy look that reflects your best self. Each step adds to your personal narrative, but here's the truth bomb; not everyone's going to hype you up. Some people can't see your growth because they're stuck replaying their own insecurities, and that's okay! Let your actions speak louder than your doubts. The glow-up is yours, not theirs. Keep leveling up, and remember: every hit series needs a slow-burn episode before the big reveal. Be patient with yourself, because your journey is worth the wait.

It is not advisable to discuss your problems with others unless you are ready to move on from them. Seeking happiness in a new love relationship while having emotional instability is a formula for catastrophe, and it should be avoided at all costs to maximize one's chances of success. This is especially true for those who are unhappy, have not recovered from prior traumas, prefer to focus on those scars, and are not yet ready to go on. These are the folks who find comfort in reliving suffering rather than focusing on how to heal and move on with their life.

It is possible that in today's culture, the reasons for many failed love relationships can be traced back to both parties' concerns. After you've solved your difficulties and released your attachments, you should present the best version of yourself to the outer world. The universe will handle the rest of the specifics if you do this.

What are the reasons that you would tell the future about your past?

a. Has this worked in your favor in the past?

Do you share bad past experiences to gain the sympathy of others? YES OR NO

Did you feel you are healed from past hurts? YES OR NO

If so, why do you choose to share or relive it with others?

...ANYTHING BUT PREDICTABLE!

Quote:

Stay private, *keep them guessing always! - Unknown*

Mystery is underrated in today's oversharing world. Think about it—when was the last time you felt intrigued by someone? Chances are, it was because they weren't laying their whole life out for everyone to see. Social media makes it so easy to document every waking moment, but the real flex? Keeping some things private. Be the person who doesn't post everything. Let them wonder what you're up to.

Maybe it's deleting that "storytime" rant or not sharing every milestone the moment it happens. Instead, live in the moment and let your growth speak for itself. Like a plot twist in your favorite TV drama, a little mystery keeps things exciting. People will lean in to know more, and you'll enjoy the freedom of living life for yourself, not for likes.

THE THRILL OF GROWTH

You know the saying: *"All work and no play makes Jill a dull girl."* Well, it's true—and let's be honest, life's too short to be boring. Sure, grinding at work or sticking to routines pays the bills, but when was the last time you truly felt alive? Life isn't about clocking in and out; it's about creating memories that make you laugh out loud during your morning coffee or inspire you to try something crazy—like slow dancing on a rooftop or starting that podcast idea you've been toying with.

Here's the deal; if you're constantly stuck in a cycle of wake, work, TV, sleep, and repeat, it's time for a vibe check. Shake things up! Book that spontaneous trip, sign up for an improv class, or get your friends together for a karaoke night. Not only will this spice up your life, but it will also remind you how important it is to balance hard work with hard play. A dynamic life isn't about being busy; it's about being engaged.

EMBRACE THE NEW

Vision board vibes, but make it real. Picture your future self: healthier, happier, doing things you only dreamed about. That's where the magic happens. Whether it's nailing that promotion, finally moving to a city you've always loved, or mastering an aesthetic Instagram feed, envisioning your ideal life is the first step to creating it.

Big life changes don't happen overnight. They start with small, consistent steps—like switching out your 2 a.m. scrolling habit for a morning journaling routine, or saying "yes" to opportunities that scare you (in a good way). Transformations are built on discipline, even if it feels slow at first. But here's the good news: every small step compounds, and before you know it, you're living a life that feels almost unrecognizable—in the best way possible.

Are you ready for a shift in your life? 

Is it time for a shift in your career? 

Are you thinking of acquiring a fresh identity in the upcoming months? 

ACTION TIME

Ask Yourself: What's one thing you've been putting off that could totally change your vibe? Is it signing up for that art class? Volunteering for a cause? Starting a new fitness routine?

Take a Baby Step: Growth doesn't require grand gestures—just one move in the right direction. DM that mentor, book the flight or apply for the gig.

Celebrate Wins: It's easy to get caught up in what's next, but don't forget to celebrate how far you've already come. Every step forward is worth a high-five (or a glass of wine).

What's hindering you from making much needed changes?

____

____

____

Which goal do you find most challenging?

____

____

____

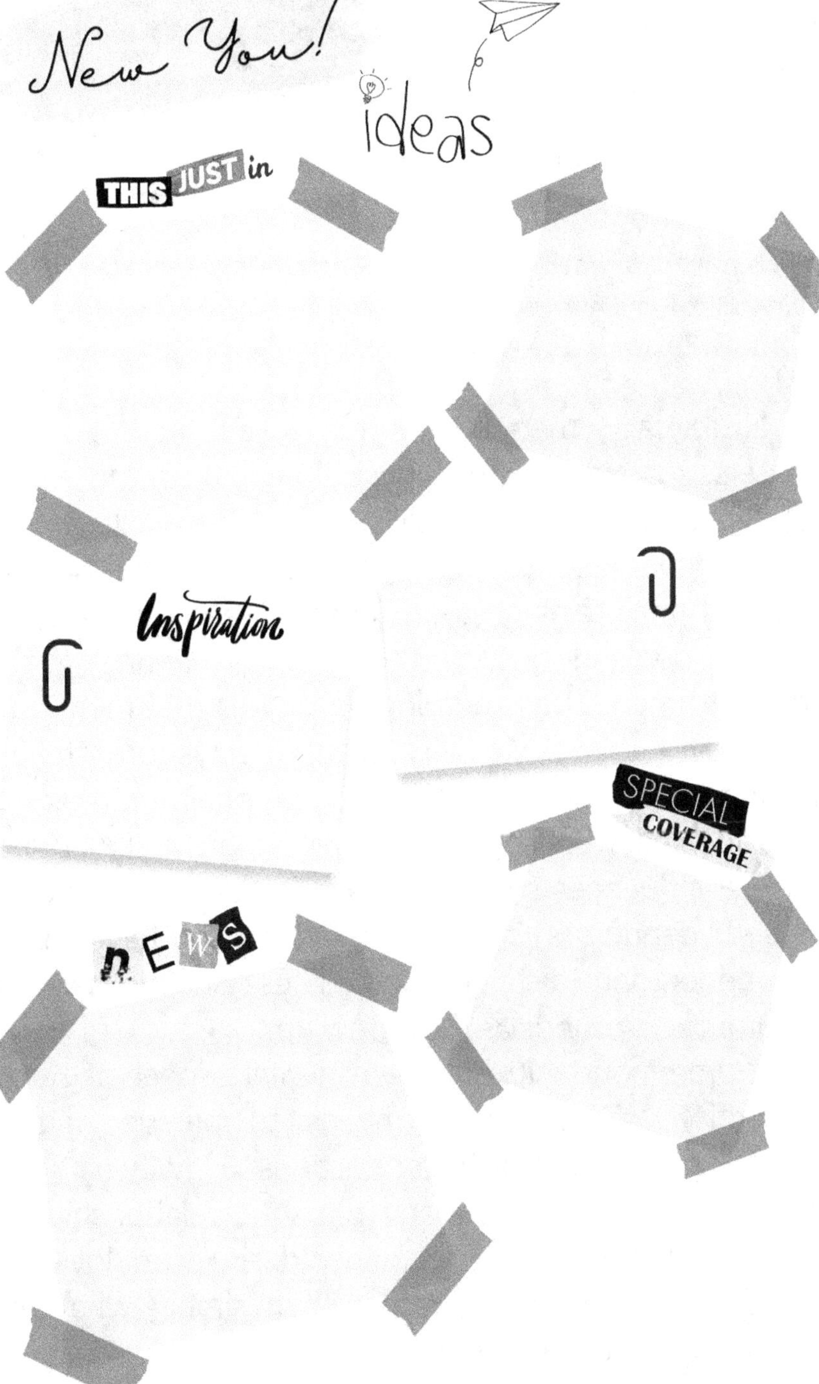
New You!
ideas
THIS JUST in
Inspiration
SPECIAL COVERAGE
nEWS

DON'T CHASE...

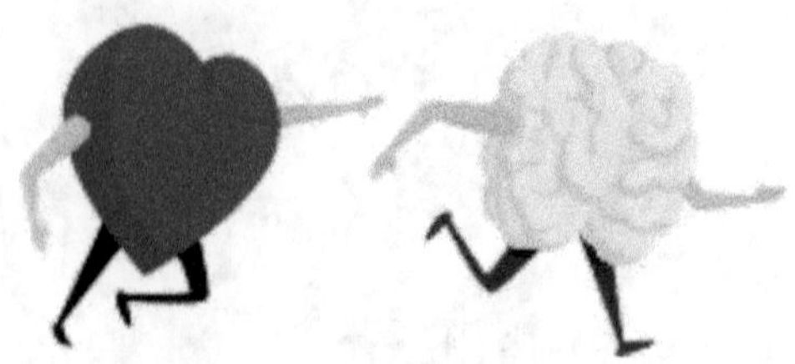

Quote:

When someone shows you who they are, believe them the first time. - Maya Angelou

FYI

Historically, men have often taken on the role of hunters, shaped by their physical attributes and societal expectations related to their gender. Meanwhile, women were encouraged to highlight their feminine qualities, such as maintaining good posture and cultivating a modest demeanor, with the goal of enhancing their appeal to men. The prevailing belief was that men would reciprocate this desirability with displays of affection, including dates, flowers, gifts, and potentially marriage.

As we mature, we gain a clearer understanding of how societal influences shape the expectations and behaviors of both genders in romantic relationships. Each gender has undergone distinct experiences, shaped by their cultural backgrounds as they grew up.

From time, courtship has been a vital aspect of human interaction, serving as a means to pursue personal ambitions and establish connections. However, recent research indicates that many romantic relationships are primarily driven by a genuine desire for love and meaningful connections, rather than simply what each partner can offer the other.

At the end of the day, while the confidence and independence that women are embracing is empowering, there's a downside. The focus on physical appearance and the pressure to conform to social media trends can overshadow what really matters in building a genuine connection. It's not that romance is dead, but it feels like finding that "perfect match" is becoming more elusive as we all play by the same rules.

DEMANDS

In today's world, the dynamics between women and men have shifted dramatically. Women are increasingly asserting themselves, no longer tolerating dismissive behavior or settling for less than they deserve. They speak up about their preferences, unapologetically acknowledging that even the most attractive men can be picky — sometimes to the point where it feels a bit shallow, especially when it comes to physical appearance.

Modern men are often drawn to women's confidence and assertiveness, seeing it as a reflection of their self-worth. This has made the dating scene feel more direct and transparent than it may have been in the past. But let's be real — men, by nature, are often driven by instinct. It's like a hunter pursuing their prey, and that primal drive can sometimes mean that women's assertiveness doesn't always lead to the lasting relationships they hope for.

When a man successfully courts a woman and earns her affection, there's often a sense of achievement — he feels like he's "won" something, which can lead to deeper commitment and better treatment in the relationship. But, of course, that's not a universal rule.

Social media plays a huge role in shaping how we see ourselves and others, especially with trends like the "baddie" or "hot girl" persona taking over. It's become common for women to lean into these trends to boost their attractiveness, hoping to stand out in a crowded online space and attract romantic opportunities.

The result? Beauty standards are being shaped more by trends than by true individuality, making it harder to distinguish between people who all look and act similarly. This has led to a space where finding a partner who feels truly unique or special is becoming rarer, as everyone is trying to fit the same mold.

HIGH-VALUE DOESN'T MEAN PERFECT

Let's debunk the myth: being "high-value" doesn't mean having it all together all the time. Perfection is exhausting, and honestly, it's not relatable. What makes you high-value is knowing your worth and being real about it. High-value people embrace their flaws while working on their growth—they're both confident and humble.

Think about it; would you rather spend time with someone who pretends to have it all figured out or someone who's honest about their journey? People are drawn to authenticity. When you accept your imperfections, you give others permission to do the same. So, whether you're rocking a messy bun at brunch or admitting you don't have a 5-year plan yet, own it. Growth is about progress, not perfection. And that's the real flex.

THE PRIZE

Here's the thing about being a prize: you don't need to announce it. True confidence doesn't shout; it glows. When you see yourself as valuable, the entire game changes. Think of it like walking into a room: are you chasing to be noticed, or does your presence naturally command attention? People notice when you carry yourself with self-respect and purpose.

Being the prize doesn't mean arrogance—it's about investing in yourself. Take care of your mind, body, and soul. Maybe that means setting time aside for self-care Sundays, journaling to declutter your thoughts, or hitting the gym to build both physical and mental strength. When you nurture yourself, you're telling the world, "I deserve to be treated well." The best part? You'll start attracting people who respect and uplift you, not because you're chasing them, but because they're drawn to your energy.

WHAT MAKES YOU THE PRIZE?

Dating has changed. Back in the day, relationships were about traditional roles. Today, it's about balance. Successful, high-value men aren't just looking for beauty —they're looking for a partner who adds value to their lives. Whether that's through emotional support, stimulating conversations, or shared ambitions, it's about finding someone who complements their energy.

This doesn't mean you need to overperform or prove yourself. Instead, focus on being your authentic self. Show up as someone who listens, respects, and inspires. The right people will see your worth without you having to convince them. And remember, being the prize isn't about outshining anyone—it's about shining in your own unique way.

THE DOWNSIDE OF CHASING

Case Study: When Giving Too Much Backfires

Have you ever been in a situation where you liked someone so much, you started bending over backward to keep them happy? Maybe you rearranged your schedule for them, ignored your own boundaries, or overlooked behaviors that didn't sit right with you. The truth is, overgiving doesn't win you love—it wins you exhaustion.

Relationships thrive on balance. If you're the only one putting in effort, it's a sign something's off. Healthy love means mutual respect, effort, and interest. It's not your job to prove your worth to someone who isn't reciprocating. Instead of chasing someone who isn't ready to meet you halfway, redirect that energy into yourself. The right person will value your efforts without you having to overextend.

Do you unintentionally fit the mold of a typical modern female? 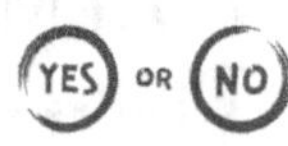

Does your appearance reflect your personality? 

Would you consider yourself a baddie? 

Would you consider yourself 'the prize'? 

Do you worry about giving too much of yourself, too soon while dating or in a relationship? 

Do you have the characteristics to be a part of a "power couple" dynamic? 

Case: 🔍

Successful men who are considered "high-value" have a reputation for being serious and dull, but they still know how to have fun. As a result, they often look for partners who are capable of fulfilling their deepest desires and fantasies. After a long and demanding day at work, these men prefer a partner who can provide them with a sense of excitement and new things to look forward to.

Conflict: ⚡

Consider what a perfect outing might entail for the average woman of the modern era. Many of today's most attractive women may give the impression of being picky, spoiled, and dominant all at once. For instance, enjoying an expensive meal at a top-rated restaurant, donning a new and alluring outfit, and capturing a great photo to share online and boast about to her circle of friends could all be examples of what she might find enjoyable and thrilling.

Case: 🔍

The majority of men prefer the process of pursuing women in a way that is not only long and enjoyable but also challenging and rewarding. This pursuit allows them to feel a sense of accomplishment and connection, as it requires effort, patience, and emotional investment.

Conflict: ⚡

Women often give men what they want too quickly, without requiring effort or proving their worth. As a result, men may lose interest over time, as they tend to value what they have to earn.

Case: 🔍
Some men appreciate intellectually engaging conversations and interactions. This means that a woman should be able to offer a range of unique perspectives on various general subjects. Knowing a variety of topics leads to stimulating conversations and fewer boring moments.

Conflict: ⚡
It's common for some people who are physically attractive to focus more on their looks than on cultivating a likable personality or way of thinking. Unfortunately, this often leads to shallow relationships that lack any real substance. This is why it's so surprising when men choose partners who aren't necessarily the most physically attractive. By looking beyond the surface, these men can find partners who possess qualities far beyond physical beauty, resulting in deeper and more fulfilling relationships.

Case: 🔍
Most successful men tend to seek companions who assist in achieving greater goals, forming a dynamic duo or power couple. While others date average women who are more submissive and reliant on them.

Conflict: ⚡
Successful individuals often exude self-assurance, which can sometimes come across as self-centered, potentially straining their relationships. The challenges of finding love are not limited to men; strong, independent women face similar struggles in today's world.

Understanding the other person's expectations early in the dating phase is crucial. Align your actions accordingly, as this will play a significant role in the relationship's direction.

VERDICT:

Ladies, it's important to approach romance with a little more logic and a little less emotion. When a guy catches feelings for you, he's naturally going to want to spend time together — but remember, you don't have to drop everything to make that happen. Set your boundaries and don't feel pressured to always be available. Also, don't bring the baggage of your past relationships into a new one. It's not fair to hold someone else accountable for things that happened before them. Instead of rushing to judge or assuming everyone's the same, take the time to get to know the person you're dating. Understand their likes, dislikes, hobbies, and what makes them tick. Ask thoughtful questions about their background, their goals, and what they're looking for. Meaningful conversations are key to connecting on a deeper level.

Most guys are pretty honest, so be ready for some straightforward opinions. And remember, if a guy is really into you, he'll put in the effort to make sure you're happy too.

ACTION STEPS FOR YOUR GLOW-UP

Assess Your Standards:

Write down your non-negotiables with a partner. Include what you need emotionally, mentally, and spiritually. Don't settle for less than what aligns with your values.

Focus on Your Value:
List 3-5 qualities that make you unique. You can empathize, with your ambition, or your sense of humor. Celebrate those traits and remind yourself why you're amazing.

Set Boundaries:
Practice saying no. Whether it's to someone who's not meeting your standards or situations that drain you, boundaries protect your peace and reinforce your worth.

How can you contribute to a relationship in a way that strengthens it or keeps it going?

Questions Women Are Asked

PRINCE CHARMING IS NOT COMING TO SAVE YOU!

Quote:

Everything that glitters isn't gold -Unknown

Nearly every child, whether at home or in school, has encountered a collection of fairy tales. In these stories, male protagonists often aspire to win the heart of a beautiful princess, while female protagonists dream of a charming and affluent hero. These narratives are a common foundation for initiating romantic relationships in today's culture, and it's easy to see why. Authors likely aimed to offer a hopeful perspective on love, relationships, and life, catering to a younger audience with optimistic portrayals.

Yet as we mature, we come to realize that these tales are largely fantasy and that we should be cautious with anything that seems too good to be true.

Even those who appear to have achieved their version of a "happily ever after" often made significant personal sacrifices to reach their current state, which to the outside world can appear perfect. The fact is there is no such thing as a perfect life, and ultimately, it is up to each of us to create the life we aspire to have, while remaining true to ourselves and others.

If fairy tales have taught us anything, it is that finding "your prince/king," especially one who is wealthy, can be difficult. While things rarely go as planned, we must always be prepared for anything that may come our way in life, including the ability to save ourselves!

FEELING FROGGY

Have you ever considered the concept of kissing a frog and how it applies to our daily lives? Despite their slimy looks and long tongues, fairytales say that if we look past these creatures' defects, we can find a gorgeous, wealthy prince waiting to be revealed. However, we immediately discovered that these notions are incorrect, and kissing a real frog, while intended to be a romantic gesture, may be quite detrimental to our health. Instead, we should simply admire frogs' intrinsic beauty for what they provide to nature in their surroundings.

Again, while frogs may not be the most appealing creatures, they are frequently used as symbols of wisdom, riches, and fortune. This serves as a reminder that we should not rely solely on appearance to form our judgment.

The Frog Prince is a timeless fairy tale that teaches us to look past the surface and value the inner beauty of all living things. After all, true beauty is within, and we should always strive to see the best in people.

Let's be real—some people still get labeled as "frogs" based on their quirks or appearance, and they often don't get the love or attention they truly deserve. In today's swipe-right culture, it's all too common to judge someone purely on their looks or their financial status. Because of this, many amazing people who have shared goals and the desire for meaningful, lasting relationships get overlooked. But just because someone doesn't fit conventional standards doesn't mean they don't have incredible qualities to offer. These individuals often understand their own shortcomings and are deeply aware of what a partner needs and wants. They're usually willing to go the extra mile to create a genuine connection that isn't based on shallow criteria.

Overlooking someone purely based on appearances or first impressions is a huge disservice—not just to them, but to yourself. Those "frogs" you might dismiss could actually be hidden gems waiting to be discovered. With love and attention, they might surprise you and turn out to be the perfect partner, capable of becoming the "diamond in the rough" you didn't expect.

Interestingly, women tend to be better at expressing what they want in a partner, while men often lean into avoiding the tough conversations or situations that come with relationships. This dynamic sometimes leads to rushing into new relationships without reflecting on past experiences.

In today's world, women have the freedom to be more selective when choosing a life partner. But this raises the big question—what qualities should a woman prioritize when looking for someone to build a future with?

ATTRIBUTES OF "PRINCE CHARMING"

- ◯ HANDSOME
- ◯ GENTLEMAN
- ◯ PERSISTENT
- ◯ CONFIDENT
- ◯ RICH
- ◯ CHARMING
- ◯ FAMILY ORIENTED
- ◯ ROMANTIC
- ◯ ASSERTIVE
- ◯ WELL DRESSED

DO YOU BELIEVE PRINCE CHARMING EXISTS? 

HAVE YOU EVER ENCOUNTERED A MODERN-DAY "PRINCE CHARMING"? 

ATTRACTIVE & SUCCESSFUL

UNATTRACTIVE & SUCCESSFUL

ATTRACTIVE & 'BROKE'

UNATTRACTIVE & 'BROKE'

OLDER MEN

YOUNGER MEN

EDUCATED
SPIRITUAL / RELIGIOUS
'MARRIED' MEN
'DIVORCED' MEN
'SEPARATED' MEN
'EXES'
ELIGIBLE BACHELORS
HUMOROUS / 'FUNNY'

Many of your responses will be based on personal experiences, which will give you a better sense of what you want or don't want when it comes to dating. If your negatives outnumber your positives, you have all the answers you need.

Notes

"SHACKING UP" 

"Why buy the cow when you can get the milk for free"

"SHACKING UP"?

The term "shacking up" is commonly used to describe unmarried couples who live together before marriage. While this phrase may be recognized in other parts of the world, it is particularly prevalent—and often frowned upon—in certain regions of the West Indies. Despite this societal approval, some parents remain strongly opposed to the practice for valid reasons.

However, many individuals have chosen to live with partners they were advised against, and some of these relationships have thrived despite warnings from family. Couples who were emotionally mature, goal-oriented, and committed to avoiding divorce had a higher likelihood of staying together, eventually marrying, and building a happy family life in their dream home.

One of my greatest joys is encouraging others to pursue their ambitions in all areas of life. With determination, effort, and a clear vision, success becomes inevitable.

TABLES TURN

Relationships of this nature often begin on a positive note, but the living arrangement can quickly unravel due to factors such as unrealistic expectations, lack of structure, poor planning, and unresolved interpersonal issues. This is especially true for couples who start living together at a young age, as inexperience and immaturity can lead to a disregard for responsibilities.

Sharing a home comes with challenges, including the need to compromise on personal space, establish boundaries, and recognize that both individuals have unique preferences, habits, and routines. If the arrangement fails, the couple may choose to move back in with their parents, as they remain legally independent and free to make their own decisions.

Even while married couples confront difficulties regularly, the pressures of their commitments to one another may make those difficulties seem even greater. Therefore, it is important for single women of any age who are in a committed relationship with someone to seriously consider the question of whether or not they could see themselves getting married to and living with the person they are dating in the future. It is in the best interest of young people to first work toward their goals as independent individuals, and only then develop attainable short-term goals, as this is the greatest way to maximize their chances of success. Two people who are successful and want to improve themselves create a more pleasant living atmosphere.

LET'S MAKE SENSE OF IT

It is reasonable to believe that if a man is willing to move in with you, he intends to remain permanently. So, why bother? Right? Is there a way to detect if you're wasting time once you've decided to do this?

Even if a man opposes marriage, he still seeks a partner who can meet his emotional, physical, and sexual requirements at home. Although it may be a selfish desire, both genders experience it in various ways.

According to studies, 80% of unmarried couples eventually split up, which means you're less than 20% likely to marry or remain with that person, even if you've been in the relationship for months or years. Women should understand the commitment that marriage necessitates in a relationship, it serves as a contract between the two parties. It is the most secure way to engage in a living arrangement with someone, particularly when there are duties associated with renting or house ownership. Nonetheless, many men try to persuade their girlfriends that they are experiencing what it's like to be married by living with them.

We see often that the lady will typically agree, and in her role as "wife-to-be," she will endeavor to impress and prove that she deserves the title. Many women eventually give up and grow disappointed after months or years of unsuccessful attempts. This is likely because the couple is acting unjustly as part of a larger psychological game.

PREMATURE

The fact that "shacking up" can result in unexpected pregnancies complicates a woman's ability to advocate for herself and set appropriate boundaries. When they have a kid or children together, she is no longer just his "significant other" or "girlfriend," but also his "baby mother" or "mother of his child." Although this appears to be useful at first glance, it has the opposite impact. In today's environment, having children for men without actual bonds can occasionally harm women, regardless of what they feel to be advantageous. Unfortunately, many guys have learned how to cheat the system, and many younger men are following suit. This trend has resulted in a large number of broken homes and fatherless children around the world.

Understanding how guys think can alter your expectations as a woman and "future wife" beyond what you've been taught. First and foremost, never compel someone to do something they aren't inclined to do. Before making decisions that will affect your emotional and physical well-being, consider all options, and do not be afraid to ask clarifying questions and address concerns.

In the end, you have complete control over the future you wish to create for yourself, as well as the goals you set. You are at your strongest when you establish self-sufficiency and confidence; this increases the possibility that a person will as a serious and stable woman and make long-term commitments with you.

Overall, you must keep your composure, patience, and tenacity in these situations; rushing into anything before time could have long-term consequences for your life.

EFFECTIVE LIVING

Only if you've tried all other options and decided that living with your significant other is the best option; here are some ideas to assist you keep the peace at home while maintaining a romantic relationship with your partner. Both couples must desire to be together and put forth the effort; otherwise, no amount of advise or suggestions will work.

- Give each other personal space, even if that means going outside to read a good book.
- Create a joint business to assist with bills.
- To keep the spark, don't get too comfortable or complacent.
- Talk to each other like you did when you first met.
- Create a game night to look forward to.
- Roleplay
- Visit or invite other couples over for drinks and a chat.
- Have discussions about trending topics.
- Start DIY projects around the house.
- Get involved in things each other enjoys.
- Go out a few times a week together and separately.
- Create a spiritual bond, and renew your faith.
- Take frequent trips together and separately.

Notes

BEFORE YOU STAND AT THE ALTER...

Quote:

"Marriage is not a solution to problems and doesn't make guarantees" - Unknown

BRAIN DRAIN

While many singles profess a desire to marry in the future, few take the necessary steps to make that goal a reality. Instead, they've settled into their single lives and are working hard to achieve their professional and personal goals.

Maybe they have grown children and are free to explore love again, but many successful, financially comfortable singles are eager to settle down and have a family. The dating pool may be restricted, but that doesn't mean there aren't any good prospects out there. This is a false assumption, and it explains why many people struggle with dating after hurtful experiences. The truth is a lot of people have inflated expectations of themselves and other people. These singles seem to be avoiding each other on purpose for reasons like mental fatigue and not wanting to put effort into relationships that don't work out.

Due to the fallout from past mistakes, a large number of individuals in their thirties and forties find themselves at the starting line. However, it seems most people would still want to try marriage once or twice if they meet someone who can make them believe in humanity again, despite all the cautions, horror stories, and bad experiences they've had. Finding your perfect partner takes time, but you shouldn't give up on it just because you're taking things slow.

TRENDS

Sadly, not every child grows up with two loving parents who can shape their views on marriage while they are impressionable and receptive. On the other hand, many adults who did not have the traditional ideals of a traditional family overcame the challenges they faced as children and went on to lead fulfilling lives.

Today, the traditional concept of a nuclear family—that is, a mother, a father, and the kids that they have—seems increasingly obsolete. Options that do not appeal only to one gender or one set of preferences have gained popularity, and this trend may be seen most clearly in the northern regions of the world.

Even though stepfamilies and nuclear families were the customary forms of family structure in the 1970s and 1980s, it is essential to keep in mind that there are many other options available today. Throughout human history, it has never been simpler to acquire a life partner and initiate a family than it is right now; whether you agree with it or not. People have chosen to find love no matter who it may be and how it looks.

However, when it comes to deciding whether or not a relationship will be able to persist with time, the single most important factor is whether or not both people are willing to commit to the path that lies ahead.

Do you feel modern men want to be married?

In your opinion, is marriage still a sacred bond?

DECISIONS

Marriage is designed to last forever, at least that is what vows indicate; therefore, those taking that leap should give the words careful consideration. Many people find it difficult to divide their attention between themselves and another person, especially if they have been single for a long period. However, it's expected that you and your spouse work together to make your union work effectively.

Despite the significance of marriage and all it represents, an increasing number of people marry for erroneous motives, like living up to society's expectations, to relieve pressures of finances, or to soothe their pain.

Getting married is a significant life decision, and you should also carefully evaluate the legal, religious, and personal ramifications before taking the plunge. Considering that you will endure the repercussions of your decision, you should trust your intuition and avoid being misled by the opinions of those closest to you. Regardless of how some people feel about marriage today, committing to give up half of your rights, space, ideas, and decisions to another person while using traditional affirmations makes for a meaningful union.

Remember that the Bible states a married couple ought to be "equally yoked," which implies they should have similar beliefs and principles on all essential issues. You should do your research on a potential spouse before getting emotionally attached to them, just like you would with a "carfax" report before purchasing an expensive item. Get to know each other's backgrounds, goals, health, criminal records, credit ratings, etc., thoroughly before you tie the knot.

Are you ready to spend the rest of your life with someone?

LOVE

By now, we've all realized that love isn't enough to keep a relationship thriving—especially something as big as marriage. The old-school ways of thinking are out the door for two big reasons: more people just aren't buying into them, and let's face it, our minds are already fried trying to juggle the chaos of modern life. There's so much more to consider—family dynamics, finances, potential challenges, and how emotionally flexible both people are.

One of the biggest reasons couples split? They didn't figure out how they wanted their relationship to work from the start. Before the wedding, it's all dreams and excitement, but after the "I do," reality can hit hard. Spending too much time together in close quarters can lead to boredom or that craving for some alone time. And if the tension builds and arguments start flying, it just pushes you both further apart.

That's why it's so important to have your own full, independent life before coming together in a marriage. It's not about each person bringing 50% to the table— it's about both showing up as 100% whole individuals.

Do you agree?   YES OR NO   *Other:* ___________________

MOST MEN OPT TO MARRY FOR ONE OF THREE REASONS BUT NOT LIMITED TO:-

Stability

The average man daydreams of settling down with a wonderful lady and raising a close-knit, happy family. Prepare mouthwatering meals for him and offer assistance in every way you can so that he may focus less on his emotional and physical responsibilities. They will want aid with making decisions, staying motivated, and concentrating on the tasks at hand in their own areas of interest. They want stability in addition to an atmosphere that is peaceful and free from conflict. A favorable self-image can be developed in a man when he experiences feelings of being liked, cherished, and understood.

Do you agree? (YES) OR (NO)   *Other:* _______________

Children

Men, on average, prefer to be married and have the stability to raise their children together rather than leave them in the hands of others. In addition, men who father children with more than one woman tend to favor the mother they believe to be the best when it comes to their children's well-being, being respectful of themselves, and their lifestyle. It's been believed that men take longer to reach adulthood than women do, thus they could go through a number of transitional phases before settling on a single goal. A man with children may decide to marry a fresh prospect and start a new family later in life if he believes she is a better fit for his needs.

Do you agree? (YES) OR (NO)   *Other:* _______________

Age

It is believed that between the ages of 25 and 35, a man's outlook on his future changes from that of a bachelor to that of a husband and father. Intelligent and accomplished young men typically picture themselves in the role of fairy tale creator. Some men don't want to settle down and have kids, preferring instead to amass as many baby mamas as they can before they officially lose their bachelor status at age 40. Even men are susceptible to the effects of their biological clock. The key difference is that they can have a say in whether or not a proposal is made, therefore they tend to use this to their advantage.

According to my observations, many guys choose to get married when they reach an age when they feel they are becoming less attractive to women. If a person's close circle of friends is all getting married, that individual may feel pressured to do the same. In doing so, they are trying to secure acceptance into the "marriage club", since is now seemingly a "cool" step.

Do you agree?   YES **OR** NO   *Other:* ___________

WHAT OTHER REASON DO YOU BELIEVE MEN MARRY?

MR. READY OR NOT!

Most guys these days think they can absolutely thrive in life without ever getting married. They're confident they've got everything they need to handle life solo and don't see marriage as a necessity. In fact, society doesn't even blink at men who marry to level up financially or socially anymore. Some guys will even openly admit that finding a partner who can contribute financially is one of their main goals—because, let's be real, the economy is wild right now. As a result, men's ideas about what makes a solid marriage are starting to align more with women's perspectives. Thanks to social media, these conversations about men stepping up their relationship standards have blown up, encouraging dudes to aim higher. But with the bar being raised, it's become way harder for women to find their version of "Mr. Right."

At the same time, many women are also rethinking their expectations, leading to a major shift in how relationships are viewed. People want partners who add value to their lives, not just someone to split the rent with. The idea of compatibility now goes way beyond romance—it's about shared goals and teamwork. Men and women alike are realizing that marriage is a partnership, not a rescue plan. And for the ones who are genuinely invested, they're approaching marriage with more thought and intention than ever before.

For guys who are genuinely hyped about getting married, you'll see it—they'll be excited and looking forward to it. If that enthusiasm isn't there, consider it a massive red flag. There's still this lingering idea that women want marriage more than men do, which is why some men think the bride deserves most of the spotlight on the big day. Many men admit their suit and their groomsmen's fits are often the only wedding details they get full control over—and they're okay with that.

A few months later, you might hear comments like, "She dragged me down the aisle!" While these remarks may be made in jest, they can sometimes reflect genuine feelings about marriage and the pressures some people experience around it.

Men who aren't mentally or emotionally prepared for marriage might perceive it as a burden, and this mindset can lead to behaviors that undermine the relationship, even unintentionally. This is why no one should feel pressured into a commitment as significant as marriage.

An unhappy spouse—on either side—may eventually have to deal with the emotional fallout of staying in a relationship that doesn't feel right. Paying attention to early warning signs is essential, as ignoring them can lead to heartache and regret down the line. Open and honest communication is key to avoiding these challenges.

Do you agree?  OR  *Other:* ______________

Is a man obligated to marry a woman he is with, within a timeframe?  OR 

Do you feel that men can be "forced" into marriage?  OR 

Do you believe men dangle marriage over the heads of women?  OR 

Should the groom assist with the planning of his wedding?  OR 

MR. & MRS. RIGHT

When two people marry and exchange vows, they do so with the intent of keeping those promises—whether or not they fully understand what it will take. These vows symbolize a commitment to working together and striving for success in both personal and professional life. Even in the face of challenges, they must remain steadfast, nurturing their bond and never giving up as they embark on life's journey together.

While love stories with happy endings may not capture as much media attention as tragic ones, they are just as real—and they offer hope to those still searching for their own. This is especially true for those raised in a home where a strong and loving marriage was present—one that left a lasting impression on their views of love and commitment. Marriage is not simply about saying "I do" once; it's about renewing, reaffirming, and revitalizing that promise every single day. If a couple wants their relationship to endure and flourish, both individuals must put in the effort to grow and evolve.

A true partner is someone who treats you with kindness, listens with care, and values you for who you are—flaws and all. On days when self-doubt creeps in, there is great comfort in knowing that someone who understands you completely will stand by your side, offering unwavering love and support. That kind of connection is rare, but it is worth waiting for—and worth fighting to keep.

Mr. or Mrs. Right will be honest with you when you're wrong, yet they will also forgive you when you make mistakes—never taking your love for granted.

This is because a true partner is not only considerate of your feelings but also eager to understand your "love languages" and how to make you feel valued.

Mr. and Mrs. Right are not perfect, but they strive to think before they act, ensuring their words and actions never bring you embarrassment or shame.

While there is no universal definition of what makes someone "marriage material," most people develop a clearer understanding of it over time. Still, a strong foundation is essential for building a healthy relationship, just as having clear criteria helps in choosing the right partner. These two elements go hand in hand, forming the backbone of a lasting and meaningful connection.

Though subjective, good 'material' consists of:

- Physically and Emotionally Supportive
- Self-aware
- Creative
- Considerate of important dates/details
- Good sense of humor
- Sex appeal
- Engaging conversations
- Helpful
- Not abusive (physically and verbally)
- Not judgmental
- Reliable
- Asks questions
- Make few assumptions
- Value's honesty
- A safe place
- Empathetic

RESPOND TRUTHFULLY TO THE FOLLOWING QUESTIONS:

Do you think you are "marriage material"? YES OR NO

Do you currently own living space? YES OR NO

Can you qualify for a family home
on your own? YES OR NO

Would you require a joint mortgage? YES OR NO

How do you feel about splitting the cost of household bills?

____

____

____

____

Do you have children from a previous relationship?

YES OR NO   If yes, how many? __________

Can your future husband have children?

(YES) OR (NO)   If yes, how many?

Are you cordial with your stepchildren's parent(s)?
If not, why not?

(YES) OR (NO) OR (N/A)

How many co-parents *(baby mothers or baby fathers)* would you be comfortable with your spouse having before it becomes a concern for you?
Explain your reasoning. #

Can outside children live in your marital home?

Are there exception(s)? Explain.

Are you prepared to be a parent to your stepchildren indefinitely? (even if separated/divorced)
Explain your decision.

Which of these motivates your desire for marriage?

- ◯ Love
- ◯ Commitment
- ◯ Wedding Day festivities
- ◯ Financial gain
- ◯ Stability
- ◯ Religious/Spiritual beliefs
- ◯ To keep your significant other
- ◯ Pressure from society
- ◯ Children
- ◯ Power
- ◯ Experience

Do you hope to have more kids at this point in your life?

(YES) OR (NO) OR (N/A)   Your age: ___________

Can you, in your current financial state, comfortably raise a child(ren) alone?

(YES) OR (NO)   How many? _________

Age? _________

Do you and your fiancé/partner currently have any children together?

What are THREE main hopes for your marriage?

1

2

3

Are you willing to make compromises in your marriage?

YES OR NO

Considering traditional vows, what are you <u>not</u> willing to compromise?

Additional Notes

Questions Women Are Asked

Rate Yourself
1-10

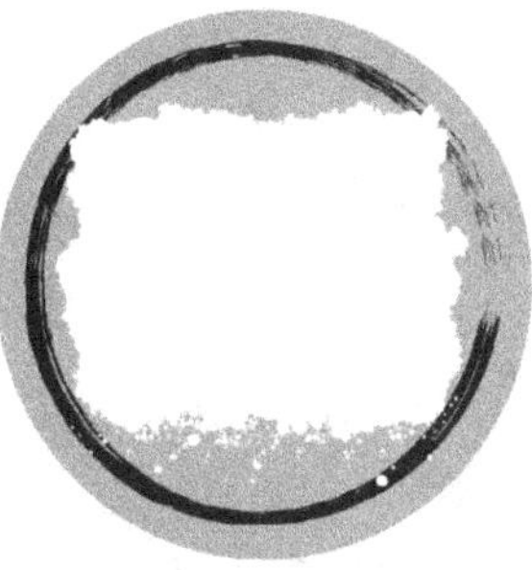

What are your
Pet Peeves?

Long, short, or no
Beard?

Your
Weakness?

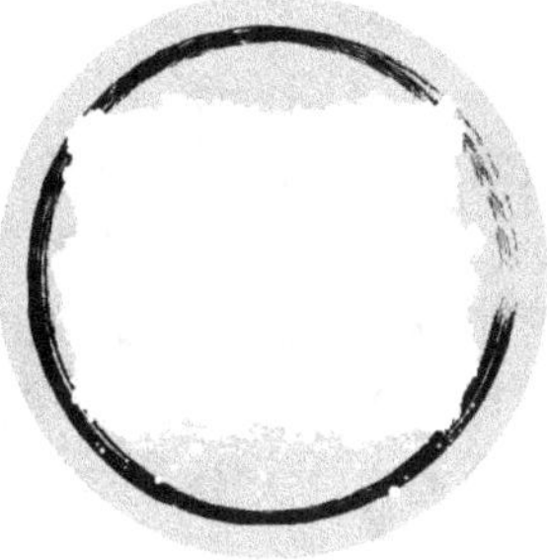

Do you
snore?

Can your man
have a female
best friend?

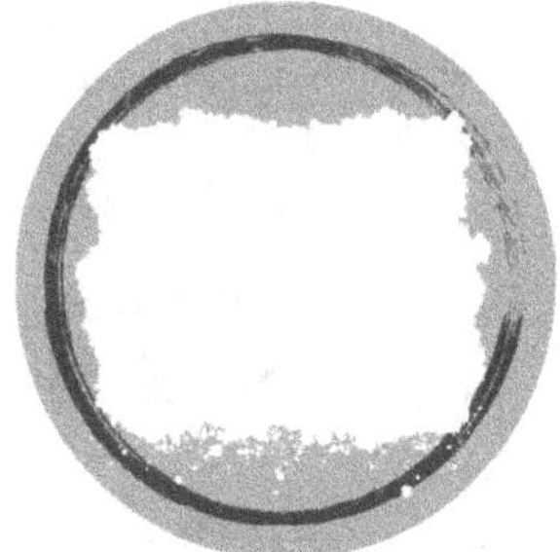

Favorite
Perfume?

Does ring
size matter?

Favorite
Cologne?

"I DO" NOT...

Quote:

"The quality of a person's life is in direct proportion to their commitment to excellence, regardless of their chosen field of endeavor." - Vince Lombardi

The real heart of a wedding isn't about the dresses, the suits, the decor, or how over-the-top the day is—it's about the genuine intentions of the couple committing to a lifetime together. It's easy to get caught up in the aesthetics and pageantry, but those things fade. What truly matters is the bond between two people and their readiness to face the ups and downs of life as partners. Wedding vows are a powerful way for couples to publicly express their dedication and set the tone for their future. However, those words only carry weight if both people act on them and remain committed to the relationship over the long haul. That's why there's so much groundwork to be done before walking down the aisle.

Couples need to take the time to work through their relationship dynamics and ensure their values align while they're still single. Open, honest conversations about non-negotiables—like ethics, lifestyle goals, and their vision for the future—are absolutely essential. Marriage proposals should be made and accepted with a full understanding of what lies ahead, not just in the excitement of the moment. Both partners should take the time to reflect on whether they're truly prepared for the emotional and practical realities of marriage.

If someone proposes before they're mentally or financially ready for such a huge commitment, they're not only fooling their partner—they're fooling themselves.

Too many couples rush into marriage for reasons like societal pressure, financial convenience, or the illusion of stability, only to find out later that they weren't prepared for the realities of married life. It's a heartbreaking cycle that drains not only their emotional reserves but also their time, energy, and finances.

Marriage isn't just a celebration or a status symbol—it's a deeply personal and life-changing partnership. Taking the time to prepare, communicate, and ensure compatibility isn't just important; it's essential to building a foundation that lasts.

VOWS

Traditional wedding vows have been around since at least the 1500s, but few people know where they actually originated or when they first became popular. Many modern couples still opt for these classic vows because they hold deep religious significance and continue to resonate in today's world. The simple words "I do" may be brief, but they carry an enormous weight. The thrill of planning the perfect wedding, the emotional highs and lows, and the electric mix of tension and excitement felt by everyone in attendance can sometimes distract from the more serious, underlying issues that even some guests might quietly notice.

These vows are more than just words—they set the tone for the marriage and, ideally, help both partners mentally prepare for what's ahead. At least, that's the hope. The reality is that many couples may not fully grasp what they're committing to when they recite these historic promises.

Let's be real: those are serious commitments! It's worth remembering that these vows were created in a time when societal roles were very different—women were far more dependent on men and had fewer options if the relationship turned toxic.

Today, while the dynamics of marriage have shifted dramatically, the weight of those words remains the same. However, it's important for modern couples to consider what those promises mean to them in the context of their own relationship, rather than simply reciting them out of tradition. After all, these vows aren't just ceremonial—they're the foundation for a lifetime of partnership. And in a world where relationships are evolving, understanding and mutual respect matter more than ever.

WOWS

The high divorce rate suggests a significant decline in the value of marriage and the commitment spouses make to one another. In the whirlwind of happiness, anxiety, and excitement surrounding a wedding, it's easy to overlook unresolved issues that may have been ignored during the planning stages. Even if some guests, including the couple themselves, sense these concerns, the event often proceeds as scheduled. It's unsettling to realize that for some, their wedding day is filled with stress, anxiety, and even fear. Yet, the focus often remains on simply getting through the day without any mishaps, embarrassment, or disappointment.

This is far from an ideal start to a marriage. It's crucial to truly understand the other person and their intentions before committing to a long-term relationship. Doing so from the outset is the best way to protect your heart and your future happiness. Despite knowing better, many women tend to overlook details and ignore red flags, often living in a "fantasy" mindset. However, it's vital to break free from this habit quickly, as repeated mistakes and inattention will eventually become evident not only to ourselves but to everyone around us.

The truth has a way of surfacing eventually, as nothing can remain hidden forever. It's crucial to pay attention to what works and what doesn't, especially since people's personalities and motivations evolve and reveal themselves over time. So, whenever you decide to say, "I do," don't assume that everything will automatically improve — in fact, it may even become more challenging. However, if you marry someone you truly know and trust, and if you are honest with yourself and your partner, your chances of a lasting, happy marriage are much greater.

Are traditional wedding vows outdated? 

Do you believe there is sincere intent behind the vows spoken? Which lines of wedding vows do you believe, and which are unrealistic?

3
Regrets:

1.

2.

3.

Notes

Notes

A FRIEND OF A FRIEND IS NOT YOUR FRIEND

Read that again...

It is not always easy to classify the people who are a part of your life, regardless of whether they are friends and coworkers, casual acquaintances, or any combination of these three types of people.

It has never occurred to me that having a single conversation with someone or spending a few enjoyable hours with them could ever replace the knowledge that comes from having years of experience and being exposed to a variety of different people and situations. Third parties, particularly those with whom the individuals involved share intimate relationships or common connections, are frequently to blame for disagreements that arise between individuals. This way too frequently.

The vast majority of the time, you will get to know these people through another person who you already know and are close to, such as a friend or relative, someone you are interested in romantically, a neighbor, or a coworker.

DO YOU KNOW SOMEONE WHO ALWAYS SEEMS TO STIR UP TROUBLE WHEN THEY'RE AROUND?　　(YES) OR (NO)

WHO AMONG THE FOLLOWING HAS BEEN THE SOURCE OF YOUR GREATEST PAIN?

☐ RELATIVE(S)　　☐ FRIEND(S)　　☐ COWORKER(S)　　☐ ASSOCIATE(S)
☐ FRIENDS OF FRIENDS　　☐ OTHER(S)

3RD PARTIES

Given that we often spend over 40 hours a week with our coworkers, it's natural to develop personal connections. Having positive relationships at work is crucial for a productive and pleasant work week. However, it's important to set boundaries to avoid conflicts between your job and workplace friendships. Maintaining a clear distinction between your professional and personal lives is essential, and these boundaries should be established from the start.

Workplace cliques can be just as damaging as those seen in middle or high school. If you limit your interactions to a small group of coworkers and don't make an effort to connect with the broader team, it can negatively impact both your productivity and overall team morale. Challenge yourself to step out of your comfort zone occasionally. While there's no risk in forming friendships with new people, it's important to remain aware of others' intentions. When joining an established group, be mindful of your role and understand that some resistance is normal. Avoid competing for approval or overextending yourself, and don't feel pressured to fit into a group that may not align with you.

CIRCLES

It would be counterproductive to express your feelings just with some of your friends and not with others. For example, if you and your closest friends have a big number of acquaintances in common with one another, discussing your feelings with only some of your friends would be counterproductive.

Some friends are indeed more close-knit than others, but you shouldn't be surprised if the knowledge you provided to one person doesn't make its way around to the rest of the group after all.

To maintain the integrity of the circle, you should hold off on making any hasty decisions until you've had some time to assess how you're feeling and whether or not something should be shared with the group. If the other individuals in the circle begin making meaningless small chats it can stir up unnecessary drama, you may sometimes need to rely on your common sense and trust your instincts. If you don't feel comfortable discussing the issue amongst yourselves, it is sometimes beneficial to have someone who is not emotionally invested in the matter to whom you can turn for advice or simply to vent your frustrations too.

As you continue to mature, you will realize that not every problem requires a reaction and even a close group of friends might experience conflict from time to time.

How to survive groups, cliques, and social circles?

Keep your word no matter what. Friends have many things in common, including these: regard, boundaries, fairness, interest, trust, honesty, care, and compassion. Particularly crucial are things like respect, boundaries, fairness, interest, and trust. If you come into contact with anything that goes against this, get rid of it immediately. On the other hand, you should always know who you are and what you stand for, keep your cool and your reputation intact, never back down from expressing your opinion, and never let anything compromise your integrity. It's not wise to stick to the same group of friends, but it is wise to surround yourself with people who value and encourage your unique qualities.

Do you have a circle of friends? 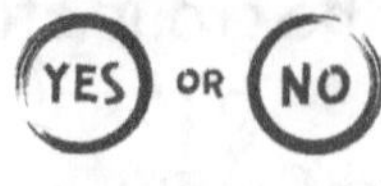

Have you ever had a conflict with a trusted friend concerning someone attached to them? 

Do you hang out with your friend's friends often? 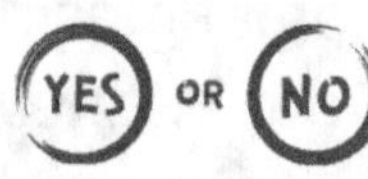

Are any of your friends' friends trouble starters? 

Have you clashed with a close coworker(s)? 

Do you have friends that gossip about their friends? 

Have you ever been a part of a work clique? 

Do you go out with any of your colleagues outside of the workplace?

Give (5) five advantages of having a close group of friends:

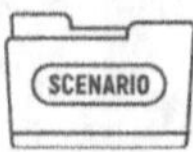

SCENARIO: The Drink Squad's Rise and Fall

Every Friday night, after a long week at work, two close friends would meet up for drinks and conversation at their favorite bar. One evening, one of them decided to invite a coworker, while the other brought along a relative who, in turn, invited a friend. The group of five hit it off immediately, sharing laughs and stories until they jokingly dubbed themselves the "Drink Squad."

Over time, the group became comfortable with each other, unintentionally sharing personal and sensitive details during their gatherings. They felt safe in this small circle, bonded by their trust and mutual enjoyment of each other's company. However, a few months later, things took a turn for the worse. An unresolved issue caused tension among the group, leading to their sudden breakup. The "Drink Squad" dissolved, leaving behind a sense of unease. Each member had been so open, believing their secrets were safe, but now they felt vulnerable, worried about how their private information might be used or spread by people they no longer trusted.

Years passed, and one day, one of the former "Drink Squad" members ran into another at a coffee shop. They recognized each other immediately, a flood of memories from their time together surfacing. As they talked, it became clear that the falling out had been based on a misunderstanding. One of them had been misled by false information, causing a rift that never needed to happen.

Realizing the mistake, they both decided to let go of the past and use it as a valuable lesson. They agreed to move on, more mindful of the importance of trust and communication in their future relationships.

Describe the lessons you can learn from the scenario?

How do you handle conflict between mutual friends?

SEE NO EVIL, HEAR NO EVIL!

Quote:

Time is the ultimate teller of TRUTHS.

HARSH REALITY

Every single one of us will be the victim of slander, name-calling, pranks, disagreements, and rumors at some point in our lives. The most painful aspect is analyzing the situation and concluding that someone you care about was involved in it. It doesn't matter if it was an intimate partner, a close friend, a neighbor, or a member of your own family; it's always upsetting to find out that someone you care about was involved.

This is something that usually catches us off guard because we were brought up to believe that those who love you would never intentionally do something to harm you. Momma never mentioned that it was actually the other way around. It is well-known that people who are very close to you have the greatest potential to hurt you mentally and physically.

In light of this, you must never forget that life is a process of determining who genuinely cares about you and who merely appears to do so regardless of who it is.

Has people close to you betrayed your trust more than (7) seven times?

MYB

Someone will constantly try to rope you into being a part of something that has nothing to do with you, even if you're just going about your day normally and peacefully. It is comparable to the biblical account of Adam and Eve when they were in the garden when all of a sudden, a serpent appeared. Most of the stories in the Bible, in my opinion, are nothing more than cautionary tales or advice for living one's life, but I digress.

But despite this, we almost always wind up being the ones who get bitten by the snakes of the world. It can be uncomfortable when someone forces you to take part in a conversation or provides you with information that you didn't ask for. This is especially true when the conversation or information includes unfavorable comments about yourself or other people, as is typically the case.

It's not hard to figure out what to do because we've all been in situations similar to the one, we're mentioning. Foresight and determination will serve you well as you prepare for the future and make strategic decisions. Be aware of the fact that so long as people continue to interact with one another, there will eventually be controversy; the key thing is how you choose to react to it when it does occur.

Do you often fall victim to the traps of snakes? 

Do you befriend people you know don't mean you well? 

BAD CONNECTIONS

It is not unheard of for people to find themselves in toxic friendships and relationships simply because they allowed themselves to become connected with the wrong kind of people. Therefore, it is crucial to carefully assess the long-term repercussions of any relationships, especially new ones. Although we strive to be decent people and give others the benefit of doubt, we must accept that evil exists in the world as we go about our daily lives.

Have you or someone you know ever engaged in unhealthy connections, leading to a downward spiral in both your personal and professional lives?
This could be something about outward demeanor, physical well-being, or general happiness.

Envy, comedy, sex, pride, wealth, and other related themes are all possible disguises that demonic spirits use to infiltrate human minds and hearts.

ENTER 5 BAD CONNECTIONS AND THE AFFECTS THEY HAD ON YOU.

CONNECTION	AFFECT

MEAN GIRLS

Hearing this phrase may give you an idea of where this conversation is going. You've most likely encountered one or more mean gals in your life. They present themselves as beautiful, kind individuals who only want to be friends with you. When these young women are not separated from the wolf pack, they feel the most secure. As young women, they quietly find flaws in you and others, propagate rumors, and exploit these flaws. Mean girls typically seek out those they perceive to be vulnerable because they are insecure themselves.

They would rarely admit that the people they regard as helpless and weak have distinguishing characteristics that they admire and as a result, they engage in clandestine attempts to acquire such characteristics. The only reason they want to befriend or become close to the individual is to obtain as much information as possible about the other person for later use. Keep an eye out for and be aware of these behaviors that are typically associated with women in a variety of social contexts, including the school, the workplace, the club, and the home.

Always select the best path for you, carefully analyze your options, exercise self-control when necessary, and listen to your inner voice. Those who initiate, disseminate, and prolong interpersonal conflict almost always struggle with or are dissatisfied with some aspect of their own life. This is true regardless of whether they are the perpetrator or the victim.

Have you ever met any mean girls in your life?   YES OR NO 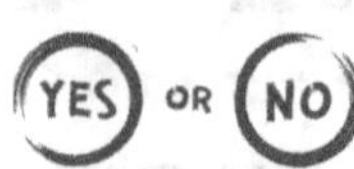

RECALL 5 MEAN SPIRITS AND THE AFFECTS

MEAN GIRLS	MEAN ACTS

CUT THE HEAD OFF

Evil usually attacks when individuals are least able to defend themselves and are most vulnerable to unsafe circumstances. You must be able to recognize them when you come across them. They struggle to build and maintain relationships with those who are helpful, self-assured, and actively interested in progressive activities regularly. Unable to see their flaws and failures, and they keep an unwaveringly negative perspective, even though their and everyone else's situations are improving. Evil is constantly involved in toxic exchanges and altercations that can be destructive to anyone who has an attachment to them. Remember that even if they appear charming to you and seek to participate in witty humor, gossip, and idle discussion, it is still founded on a spirit of negativity that is transcending in yours.

It is critical to cut ties with folks who drain your energy and negatively alter your aura, and to understand that allowing these people into your life is asking for disaster in the future. Surrounding oneself with positive, enthusiastic people who share one's love for the finer things in life and the aesthetic worth of things like art, music, and, most importantly, light is the most efficient strategy for personal growth and defense against bad forces.

WHAT DID YOU LEARN FROM ALL OF YOUR VARIOUS EXPERIENCES?

HIGH-VALUE WOMAN?

Quote:
Be the girl you want your daughter to be.
Be the girl you want your son to date.
Be classy, be smart, be real, but most importantly
be nice. Germany Kent.

Isn't it true that women are held to unfair standards by society? She is expected to be a 'Superwoman' in many ways—'Supermother', 'Superwife', 'Supergirlfriend', 'Superbest friend', 'Superemployee', and above all 'Supervirtuous' and near perfect before being eligible for a marriage proposal.

Though Momma said life isn't easy, some nuggets can help you navigate the world of interpersonal relationships more effectively.

THE STANDARD

A confident woman, regardless of size, shape, or race, is respected by a guy. A lady with a lot of energy is fun to be around because she appreciates new experiences and is always up for a new adventure.

Her curiosity and connection with the world make her an engaging person, and she constantly appears joyful and upbeat. She is not clinging to anything and maintains a sense of balance in her activities.

She does not believe in fairy tale dreams; rather, she makes her dreams come true. She has a great sense of humor but can transition to serious mode when necessary. She is perceptive and self-assured and never backs down.

She is financially independent, fiercely self-aware, and a capable and nurturing caregiver for the family, particularly her children, which most great men value. Her presence and personal touches will transform a house into a home.

She is equally willing to assist her partner with his work, even if it is as basic as handing him his tools or offering emotional support. This demonstrates that she is helpful and concerned.
Someone with good character would want to keep that kind of gal, she's no doubt a keeper! but who is this kind of gentleman who deserves such a gem?

Many men have personality defects that lead them to take advantage of the women they know. It's unfortunate, but women should always maintain their dignity, and independence even in the face of hardships. Never settle for less than you deserve, wait for a man who is willing to meet you on your terms based on good morals and standards, instead of lowering yourself to his level.

In this survey, ask your partner to answer **YES** ✓ or **NO** ⊗ if they feel you possess any of the High-Value attributes below.

WHICH HIGH-VALUE ATTRIBUTES DO YOU POSSESS? ✎

- ○ **Beautiful**
- ○ **Physically fit**
- ○ **Well-dressed**
- ○ **Submissive**
- ○ **Cooks**
- ○ **Job**
- ○ **Emotionally balanced**
- ○ **Business Owner**
- ○ **Honest**
- ○ **Intelligent**
- ○ **Forgiving**
- ○ **Financially stable**
- ○ **Sexy**
- ○ **Cleans**
- ○ **Self-aware**
- ○ **Confident**
- ○ **Self-sufficient**
- ○ **Spiritual**
- ○ **Mentally stable**
- ○ **Supportive**
- ○ **Observant**
- ○ **Thoughtful**

____ / 22

✎ MAKE THE CONNECTIONS

A HIGH-VALUE WOMAN:

Invests in	BOUNDARIES
Knows her	RESPECT
Growth	HERSELF
Surrounds herself with	WORTH
Sets	MINDSET
Demands	VALUABLE PEOPLE

What are your views on the concept of "High Value"?

NEVER MAKE YOURSELF AVAILABLE TO EVERYONE - ALL THE TIME

Quote:
Absence makes the heart grow fonder!

It is true that keeping promises to key people in your life, whether it's about money, emotions, or time, can provide you with a sense of fulfillment. However, much like a traditional bank account, there should be limits on withdrawals and monitoring of deposits made in your life. You should never feel forced to be available at any time of day or to anyone who approaches you. Establishing healthy and realistic limits is critical for protecting your time, energy, and emotional well-being.

It's not unreasonable to expect others to support you if you have gone out of your way to make time and accommodate their demands. Some people believe in the law of karma, that helping others increases the likelihood that they will be helped in return. While this may be true, it does not mean you should rush to fulfill everyone's expectations, especially if it causes you grief or a setback in your own life.

Without much thought, it is common to say things like "Call me if you need anything" or "I'm always here for you" to show support. However, these statements can sometimes create problems. Firstly, they can lead to disappointment and misunderstandings. Secondly, they may allow others to take advantage of the situation.

DO YOU SOMETIMES FEEL YOU ARE TOO NICE?   YES OR NO

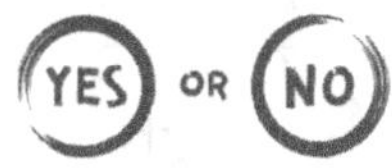

When others are vulnerable or need help, you should be careful about what you say to them at that moment, particularly if you are preoccupied with your own urgent matters. Many people pay attention to what you say and hold you to it, therefore make no commitments you can't keep. Even though most people intend well, we should all be careful with the words we choose to express ourselves.

It's essential to keep your doors open to those who truly value you and appreciate your company. While not everyone thinks and behaves the same way you do, a small percentage of the population is always willing to prioritize other people's needs and make adjustments accordingly. Such selfless acts require tremendous mental and physical strength, but the rewards are sometimes not reciprocated.

As you journey through life you will see the importance of investing in yourself, which is the key to unlocking a brighter future for you and those around you. Learning how to thrive after marriage and motherhood can open up endless possibilities. As a parent, it's easy to feel like you need to be strong and present in every way for everyone else. However, it's crucial to remember that anything overused is bound to get damaged. Therefore, it's vital that you take care of yourself, so you can continue to be a positive influence on those around you.

TAKE A BREAK

Taking weekly strolls, or catching a ride with friends, or a significant other, can be an excellent way to unwind and appreciate the journey. It's essential to remember that asking for help is not a sign of weakness, but rather a sign of strength.

If you are always willing to assist others, don't hesitate to reach out to your extended family or "village" for support when you need it. Remember, a strong support system is key to a happy and fulfilling life.

Discovering your interests, objectives, hobbies, and other activities that you like may have a positive impact on your mental health in different ways. When you reach a new level of success, you should pause to think about all you've done to get there and how far you've come. Honor your accomplishments and give others the space and freedom to do the same for you without putting undue pressure on them.

Are you feeling overwhelmed and in need of a break?

Take the time to leave your house at least once a week, even if it's just for a short while. Whether you prefer to go solo or with a group, this change of scenery can work wonders for your well-being. Maybe you are concerned about the cost of a getaway. Consider staying with a friend or relative instead. Remember, time outside of work is precious and should be used wisely. Set aside some time to relax with a good book in a quiet spot in your home or yard. And don't forget about the benefits of socializing with others. Joining clubs or organizations that interest you can help you hone your people skills. And if you need to, don't hesitate to turn off your phone for a few hours and take a break from being constantly available. You deserve it!

LIST TWO PEOPLE WHO TEND TO TAKE YOUR KINDNESS FOR WEAKNESS:

______________________________   ______________________________

LIST TWO PEOPLE YOU CAN DEPEND ON:

______________________________   ______________________________

ARE YOU TOO AVAILABLE?

- [ ] You're always the one offering advice and recommendations.
- [ ] You are always ready for whatever they have in mind. "Yes-person"
- [ ] You put a person's needs, wants, and family ahead of your own.
- [ ] They dictate or involve you without your consent.
- [ ] People depend on you, even for little things.
- [ ] You don't mind if they contact you whenever.
- [ ] You have no choice but to be there for them.
- [ ] You frequently sacrifice your plans for others.
- [ ] You never want to miss a call.
- [ ] You can't focus on "you" because of others.
- [ ] They only contact you in emergencies.
- [ ] You've told them too much about yourself, now they know everything about you.
- [ ] You're interrupted mid-sentence and ignored.
- [ ] You would drop whatever you were doing and rush to answer a message.

FOOD FOR THOUGHT!

Quote:
A woman who can't cook is as useless as a man who can't fix things
- Ms. Moonlight Stories

These days, food is more than just fuel—it's an experience, a vibe, and often the centerpiece of our social lives. We're all on the hunt for the next best bite, whether it's a hole-in-the-wall taco spot or a viral TikTok recipe. But let's be real—many of us say, "I can't cook" or "Cooking just isn't my thing." That's fine, but here's the catch: being able to cook isn't just a skill, it's empowerment. Whether you're flying solo, sharing a space with roommates, or thinking about your future self (or family), knowing how to throw together a decent meal is a game-changer.

The good news? Cooking doesn't have to feel like a chore. There's a world of resources to make it accessible and fun. Start with YouTube; it's packed with creators who make cooking feel less like a science experiment and more like a hangout. And don't sleep on cookbooks! While some look intimidating, plenty are beginner-friendly and packed with recipes that'll leave you saying, "Wait, I made this?"

Growing up, I watched homemakers in my family work tirelessly to keep everyone fed, often treating cooking as a duty. While I respect that perspective, I've learned to see cooking differently—as a form of self-care, creativity, and connection. So, whether you're chopping veggies to your favorite beats or mastering a one-pot pasta, remember: cooking is a skill anyone can learn, and it'll pay off for the rest of your life.

I'm no "Iron Chef," but I can throw down in the kitchen when the moment calls for it. I'm also not a hardcore "foodie" like half the people on my Instagram feed, but I can still whip up some fire meals that keep me and my people happy and healthy.

When life gets hectic (which is most of the time), I stick to my go-to recipes—quick, easy, and still packed with flavor. And whether or not you've got kids, paying attention to what's on their plate matters. Once you get the hang of things, cooking doesn't feel like such a chore—it's more like a life hack.

Bake It Till You Make It

Learning to cook and bake is a solid life skill for everyone, not just the Pinterest-perfect crowd. Get your little ones involved early with mini kitchen sets or kid-friendly tools—it's cute and productive. Not feeling inspired? Hit up the culinary pros in your circle for tips. And if you want to spice things up (pun intended), challenge your partner or family to a cooking battle— the winner gets bragging rights and dessert.

Pro tip: food isn't just fuel; it's a love language. Sharing a meal can fix even the most awkward family dynamics— trust me, I've seen it happen. Plus, knowing how to cook is a flex for everyone, not just women. A home-cooked meal made with care? That's a vibe anyone can appreciate.

Women Know What's Up

Let's put this out there: the whole "women can't decide what to eat" line is tired. We know what we want— pass the guac, and keep it moving. So let's drop the old-school stereotypes. We ladies are just as solid as guys when it comes to making decisions. Our choices aren't random; they're backed by thought and intention.

Want to get a feel for someone's personality and vibe? Just ask about their favorite spots to eat or grab a drink. It's a fun way to connect, but honesty is key—sharing your real preferences makes getting to know each other so much better.

Now, let's keep it real: sometimes, women hesitate to pick a place to eat. Not because we don't know what we want, but because there are so many options. Plus, a lot of us instinctively consider what our partner might enjoy too. Balancing kindness with what we genuinely want can feel tricky, but it's so important to speak up and own our choices.

Here's the tea: guys love good food and chill vibes just as much as we do. Trying out new spots or revisiting faves is their jam—especially when it's with someone they care about. Instead of buying into the tired "women don't know what they want" narrative, let's flip it. Women deserve the space to explore and express what makes them happy, including where and what to eat.

For women, being upfront about what you're craving (while keeping your partner's taste in mind) makes dining out more fun and way less stressful. No one's a mind reader, and honesty just makes things smoother.

With a little patience and a lot of understanding, dining out can be a win-win for everyone. Let's ditch the idea that women are indecisive and start hyping them up to make bold, confident choices.

Food isn't just about filling up; it's about sharing laughs, making memories, and vibing together. So, speak your truth, enjoy the process, and make every meal an adventure you'll never forget.

Do you agree?   (YES) OR (NO)

Do you enjoy cooking? (YES) OR (NO)

Do you cook more than two (2) times per week?   (YES) OR (NO)

WHEN ASKED, AND YOU ARE UNSURE WHAT TO EAT, IT'S FOR THESE REASONS:

- ☐ BRAIN FREEZE
- ☐ THINKING ABOUT PROXIMITY
- ☐ CONSIDERING YOUR PARTNER'S FOOD TASTE
- ☐ BEING MODEST
- ☐ PICKY EATER
- ☐ I ALWAYS KNOW WHAT TO EAT
- ☐ OTHER:

DO YOU ENJOY COOKING?   (YES) OR (NO)

DO YOU ENJOY BAKING?   (YES) OR (NO)

ARE YOUR KITCHEN SKILLS YOUR BEST ASSET?   (YES) OR (NO)

WOULD YOU SELL YOUR FOOD AS A PROFESSION?   (YES) OR (NO)

DO YOU COOK OR EAT OUT MOSTLY?   (YES) OR (NO)

FAVORITE MEALS

★
★
★
★

FAVORITE PLACES TO EAT

★
★
★
★

COMFORT FOODS

★
★
★
★

CRAVINGS

★
★
★
★

LET YOURSELF OUT!

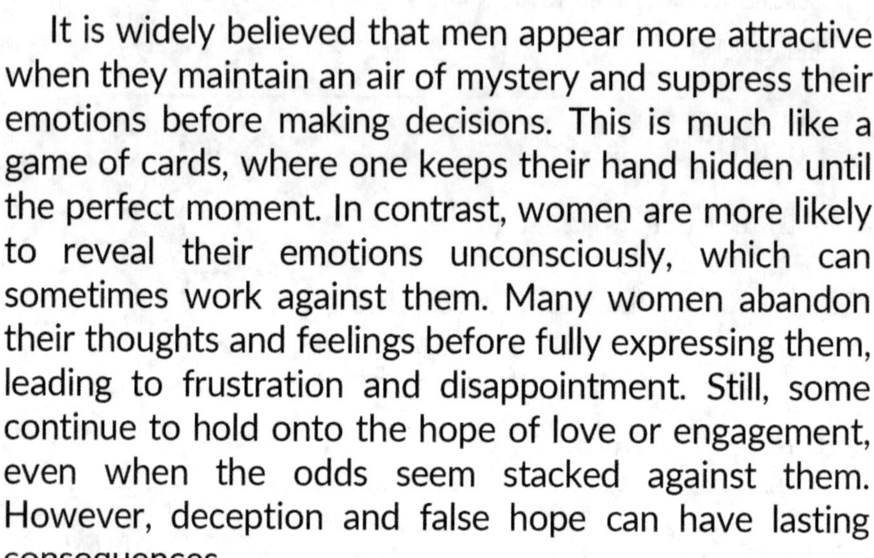

Quote:
"Time and tide wait for no man" - Ancient Proverb

It is widely believed that men appear more attractive when they maintain an air of mystery and suppress their emotions before making decisions. This is much like a game of cards, where one keeps their hand hidden until the perfect moment. In contrast, women are more likely to reveal their emotions unconsciously, which can sometimes work against them. Many women abandon their thoughts and feelings before fully expressing them, leading to frustration and disappointment. Still, some continue to hold onto the hope of love or engagement, even when the odds seem stacked against them. However, deception and false hope can have lasting consequences.

It's easy to become so caught up in the moment that months—or even years—pass by without giving much thought to your dating or romantic life. If this has happened to you, there are ways to ensure it doesn't happen again. Those who have gone through it often describe it as a terrible experience. Since we cannot change the past, the best we can do is learn from our mistakes and set more practical, achievable goals for the future. Ultimately, though, the main focus should be on identifying the root cause of the issue and addressing it.

Before analyzing the situation, let's try to understand the person's motivations and inner thoughts. Keep in mind that if you allow someone to treat you badly or bring you down in value, you could be seen as complicit. The sayings "You get what you deserve!" and "A person will only treat you how you allow them to treat you." are common knowledge. These are two well-established facts, but many other factors influence people's actions, both good and bad, and most of these can be studied and understood. People may use manipulation to get what they want, keep their pride in check, or avoid accountability for their actions. They may feel the need to control or punish their friends, or they may simply want others to feel sorry for them.

Trying to teach a manipulative person a lesson is pointless because they won't change their behavior. If you come across someone who thrives on your frustration and bewilderment, you might be walking into a trap. Manipulative people may try to gain emotional power over you by making you feel like you have a lot in common approving of everything you do, and then using your vulnerabilities to control you. If you find yourself interacting with a manipulative person who insists on making your life miserable no matter how much you try to avoid them, it's time to go on the offensive. You can defend yourself from manipulators by deciding what you stand for and sticking to it, no matter what.

Manipulators use consistency to keep you trapped in their control. To avoid falling prey to manipulation, you must actively resist the limits people place on you. You are the best judge of what is best for your own life because no one else understands you or your situation as well as you do. Never settle for less than you feel you deserve, and don't conform to other people's limits.

LOVE VS. "IN LOVE"

"Love" is a feeling that can be felt in a wide range of human interactions, including romantic and platonic ones. Being "in love" is similar to having a crush in that it is defined by a deep emotional and romantic attachment to another person. Unlike falling in love, which is a transient sensation that can either end or intensify over time, loving someone can endure your entire life. When you are "in love" with someone, you have an incomprehensible desire for intimacy with them. You have a strong need to be near them, and they are on your mind and in your thoughts throughout the day.

As you grow older, you are exposed to a broader spectrum of emotions, including many sorts of love. You will have a better knowledge of how humans function as a whole and how our emotions influence our behavior.

"I love you" Unconditional agape love can be translated as "I care about you" or "I care about what happens to you." This is a normal emotion shared by all members of the human race. However, depending on the interactions that occur, the strength of one's feelings of love may increase or decrease.

When some people experience the sensation of their current level of happiness, they may express their feelings by saying, "I love you."

Other people may say "I love you" when they recall their previous level of happiness. There's also "I love you," which was originally a powerful sense of attraction and closeness but can be transformed back to agape, as in "I love you, but I want what's best for you, even if it means we're no longer together." Many individuals may find that love that is conditional on particular factors is temporary and puzzling.

Many times, people will use justification to defend why they love another person, especially if they believe they are unable to live without that other person simply because of how they changed their perspective on life.

What has been your worst experience?

Why a man might manipulate or string you along:

○ **Casual.**
Some males may desire the benefits of being in a relationship without the associated obligations, especially marriage and children. This may indicate a lack of maturity; but, if all he wants is friendship and sex, he may not mind stringing you along until you put an end to it.

○ **Rebound.**
This is maybe the most difficult form of relationship to grasp. You will, however, notice warning signs, especially if he recently ended a long-term relationship or has been divorced. At this juncture, most males feel bewildered as they try to fall in love again. He may be unintentionally tying you up since he isn't ready to commit but also doesn't want to be alone. Don't allow yourself to be taken advantage of.

○ **Undecided.**
It may be difficult to admit, but he may not be that interested in you. He may enjoy certain elements of you, but not enough to be exclusive or committed. Some people are unsure whether a long-term relationship is in their future; therefore, they will strive to make that decision every day. Assist him in making a decision!

○ **Jerk.**
An honest companion would not string you along or ignore what you are experiencing. Sincere people rarely behave in this manner; instead, they follow the Golden Rule and treat others as they would like to be treated. However, because some individuals are jerks, they are less likely to care how their actions affect the feelings of others.

○ **Ego.**
Some men seek affirmation from playing with any woman, regardless of her attractiveness to them. If a man is able to influence you, he will eventually take control of the relationship. It's for his own good, among other reasons, so please don't take any of them lightly. The need for the validation that comes from being desired shows how insecure this individual is.

KEEP SECRETS TO YOURSELF...

If You Don't Want Them Heard Again!

Quote:

"How can we expect another to keep our secret if we cannot keep it ourselves." –François de La Rochefoucauld, Maxims

Nobody shares everything about themselves, regardless of who they are or where they come from. Depending on the specifics of the situation, we reserve the right to take whatever measures we believe to be necessary to protect the confidentiality of our information. Let's keep things in perspective; there are various secrets someone can maintain and various reasons they can choose to reveal them. While I agree that we should always be honest, I also think it's important to consider the views of the people closest to us before making a call. Both the truth and a secret can be painful, but which would cause more harm?

Each person's life and future are affected in their unique ways, therefore, it's important to treat each issue individually and do what's best for the person or people involved, even you. On the other hand, as we grow older, we learn that it's not always a good idea to confide in the first sympathetic ear that supplies one. Disappointment from loved ones happens all the time. The likelihood that someone may reveal private information during an argument depends on how much they value privacy. After seeing this happen multiple times, I think sometimes it's better to finally put it to rest.

If you feel it's better off left in the grave, leave it there, however; there are always old skeletons that resurface, and one must be prepared for if and when they do. Everyone has their methods for coping with the pressures of secrecy. For a long time, people have been honing their skills at keeping their personal information secret. You are the only one who knows the reason why you haven't disclosed this knowledge yet, and it may be because you don't think it's important and nobody cares, or it could be because you're scared about what other people will think of you. In the end, I think that even the most shameful of our deepest, darkest secrets wind up becoming a part of who we are.

The "most damaging secrets" are often ones that have been concealed from the general public for an exceptionally extended period of time. Patients and workers often feel the most at ease opening up about challenging issues during the first session with a therapist or counselor, regardless of whether the session takes place in a clinical or corporate context. An initial degree of safety is given to you due to the fact that they are people you do not know personally. As a result, they are less likely to divulge any information that you offer to them. It has been shown that a person's sense of identity is both strengthened and protected when they keep their deepest, most personal ideas to themselves.

You will ultimately feel as if the secret is ingrained in every part of your existence. In point of fact, we are the only ones who can ensure our own safety by ensuring that none of our secrets are shared with anybody else. You shouldn't give out any personal information until you reach a point where you are comfortable doing so. However, if you don't feel like you're ready to take that step just yet, that's just OK!

Will you take your deepest secrets to your grave? 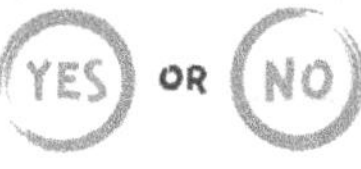

What is your motivating factor?

TOXIC ISOLATION!

Quote:
People will never forget how you made them feel
*   -Maya Angelou*

NEW CAR SCENT

Whether or not they are conscious of the tendency, there is a subset of women who have an unfortunate propensity to isolate themselves in romantic relationships. You see them one minute, they phone or come to visit you the next, and they have no time for anything but one thing. Everything changes and moves to accommodate the one person they're seeing and the activities they share together. This is not limited to romantic relationships; it may also be seen in platonic friendships. Given that we all require aid from others at some point, this is neither healthy nor constructive in a professional relationship.

Furthermore, it disrupts the balance that is required for regular functioning. Toxic and unhealthy conditions that emerge in human interactions may be difficult to resolve. When one is convinced that their partner or best friend is the only person who truly cares about them, they are more likely to cut themselves off from their extended family and other friends. People that exude toxic traits often seek out victims and act out those traits, which might include being disrespectful, angry, defensive, and withdrawn. In severe circumstances, abusive spouses will actively isolate their partner from their support system since doing so gives them more control over the relationship and the survivor.

Although these circumstances typically require intervention, occasionally a person "wakes up" to their situation on their own as they get older. When they're behaving in a way that's authentic for them again, this can easily be seen as self-centered and unfair.

If you ever find yourself in this position, remember the people who helped you through the difficult moments. Putting the future of a friendship or family bond in jeopardy because of the temporary perfection of a scenario is a bad idea. Immediately begin making preparations to restore broken connections and lines of communication.

Another component of toxic isolation exists. This occurs when women isolate their male partners from other individuals, particularly other women. The reason for this can be:

1. *To discourage them from cheating.*
2. *To Prevent them from seeming attractive to other women during travel, work, church, social gatherings, and parties.*
3. *To keep their tunnel vision on them and them alone.*

Sometimes women will even try to tell men when they can and can't spend time with their loved ones. Such behavior is symptomatic of a poisonous mindset, which is in turn connected to insecurity and the fear of being rejected. If you find yourself engaging in this behavior, remind yourself that it serves no useful purpose and won't last. Adults will do what they want, whether it's in your face or behind your back. Honor a man's honesty and sincerity, and avoid manipulating him into lying by constantly badgering him.

Men love self-assured women because they find it motivating to see such commitment, and they find it attractive to do so. Take advantage of the time that your partner is gone to do some reflection on your own life and perhaps even make something particularly thoughtful ready for him to present to you when he returns from his trip. You could try this out rather than focusing all of your attention on what he is doing instead.

DO YOU KNOW ANYONE DISPLAYING TOXIC ISOLATION PATTERNS? 

HAVE YOU EVER SHOWN TOXIC ISOLATION? 

HAS SOMEONE EVER ALIENATED YOU FROM YOUR LOVED ONES? 

DOES YOUR SIGNIFICANT OTHER CRAVE YOUR COMPANY MORE THAN USUAL? 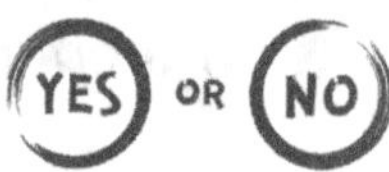

DO YOU HAVE CLINGY A FRIEND(S)? 

WOULD OTHERS BE JUSTIFIED IN IGNORING OR NEGLECTING SOMEONE WHO IS ISOLATING THEMSELVES? 

Notes

OLDER MAN < YOUNGER WOMAN

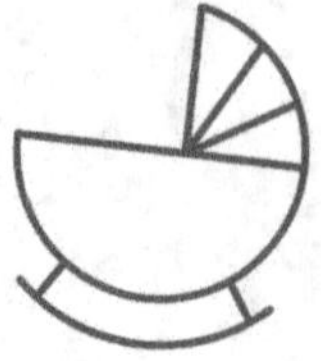

Quote:

"The Hand That Rocks the Cradle Is the Hand That Rules the World" - William Ross Wallace

CONTRACT

Let's face it—while men have historically been drawn to younger, more energetic women, it's becoming increasingly common for older men to date or marry women closer in age to their kids. On the flip side, some younger women are attracted to older men, often seeing them as a financial safety net or a source of stability. It might seem like an uneven trade, but there's usually an unspoken agreement at play—each has their own goals and objectives. But the real question is: at what cost?

It's no secret that some men, the moment they start seeing those first grey hairs, ditch their families to chase a second youth. For decades, they've been fantasizing about women who look like the ones they've admired on TV or in magazines, so it's no surprise they pursue that image when given the chance. While this behavior isn't shocking for men in general, it's particularly striking in older men, who seem set on spending their later years living out their wildest dreams—no matter how amazing or disastrous that decision might be!

DID YOU EVER DATE A MAN 12 YEARS YOUR SENIOR OR OLDER?   (YES) OR (NO)

HAVE YOU DATED A MAN YOUR FATHER'S AGE?   (YES) OR (NO)

TERMS

Whether or not you agree with it, men have an insatiable desire for excitement, and they are willing to spend a lot of money to satisfy that urge. Among these extreme methods, this gives these guys a sense of pride by permanently establishing their claim to their investment as the exclusive and sole proprietors, or so they think? However, many women older and/or married of his generation have been condemned for being too boring and uninteresting in the bedroom and for not making as much of an effort with the upkeep of their physical appearance as they once did.

They also feel women older can be a bit opinionated, demanding and individualistic. This is comprehensible when taking into account the continual difficulties that average women face while trying to balance their job, family, and childcare responsibilities. Ironically, few wives receive little to no assistance with these day-to-day activities, and even fewer are given money to treat themselves to a day at the spa or a shopping spree as a reward for meeting their daily obligations. No matter what she says, or looks like in his eyes, he may still decide he wants someone other than the woman he is with.

It is true that everyone has their own life to live as well as their own personal tastes, and it seems men and even women prefer a life with fewer questions, obligations, and barriers. However, when making decisions, it is always essential to consider others who are affected.

CLAUSE

Young ladies today must realize there is a cost to a carefree existence packed with adventure and extravagant presents. No one, regardless of age or status, should ever exploit them sexually or wear them as trophies. A young woman has the maximum amount of time to plan the path that will influence the remainder of her life between the ages of 18 and 30.

You will find out that many unsuitable partnerships have long-term adverse effects on the wellness and contentment of the body and mind of both persons involved in the relationship. Even though this is not the case in every instance, a significant number of these linkages do not care about the effects of the pressure placed on one another, since realistically both individuals are interested in having their individual wants satisfied.

A younger women, in contrast to men twice their age with more life experience, are more likely to form deep bonds quickly. While there is no such thing as permanent happiness, our bodies go through various changes as we age, some of which can be rather unpleasant. She may soon discover that a man's age undoubtedly plays a role in his sexual performance, which may prevent her from feeling satisfied and exploring other alternatives. At this point in life, women tend to prefer sexual partners who are closer to their age. To get what he wants when he wants it, the man will shell out cash for a younger woman. Unfortunately, feelings of bitterness, envy, and rage can develop from a false sense of entitlement. Given that it was designed to fall short, one would expect undesirable results. You'd do yourself a favor by avoiding these connections and instead working on developing your independence and confidence.

Always keep in mind that attractiveness diminishes, that nothing in life comes for free, and that the only things that truly endure are genuine love, dedication, trust, and friendships built on mutual respect; these are the components that make life worth living.

WOULD YOU SAY THAT YOU HAVE "DADDY ISSUES"?   YES OR NO

DO YOU FEEL LIKE YOU WERE UNDER THE CONTROL BY AN OLDER MAN YOU DATED?   YES OR NO

WERE YOU HAPPY WITH YOUR SEXUAL EXPERIENCES?   YES OR NO

WERE YOU TREATED WITH RESPECT?   YES OR NO

WOULD YOU CONSIDER MARRIAGE WITH SOMEONE MORE THAN HALF YOUR AGE?   YES OR NO

What lessons did you gather from your past encounters?

"SINGLE MOM/DAD" BADGE OF HONOR?

Quote:
"Refuse to inherit dysfunction. Learn new ways of living instead of repeating what you lived through." – Thelma Davis

PHENOMENON

I have always been curious about different cultures and lifestyles, particularly familial traits. While many fathers and grandfathers are exemplary figures, it's unfortunate that many children, both in the past and present, grow up with fathers who are either absent or play a minimal role in their development. Although men are sometimes blamed for their absence at social events for their children, their demanding work schedules may be seen as valid reasons for not being more involved.

Historically, women have been essential in providing for families, both financially and emotionally. Many men acknowledge this, often recognizing that they were raised by hardworking single mothers.

To better understand this issue, I chose to focus on the character flaws and emotional factors that contribute to the recurring breakdown of family relationships.

Women, and mothers in particular, must pause and reflect on why we keep putting ourselves in situations where we wind up with children, often multiple children by different men, and often children by men who are called "deadbeats." You may find that many guys who display commitment problems have unresolved issues with their fathers if you dig a little further. There will always be an outlier or two, but women rarely choose guys with established families and strong interpersonal relationships.

Regardless of whether or not males want to take part in pregnancy and childrearing, women nonetheless have the primary responsibility for these duties. Women are often expected to do more than their fair share, which can lead to resentment and resentful offspring.

SINGLE WOMAN VS. SINGLE MOM

It is crucial to define "single mother" because there are numerous types of mothers that fit into this classification. A "single mother" is now described as a woman who raises her child or children without the assistance of the child's father or another male figure, and who has little or no relationship with the father. Her lifestyle would be altered if she had to work more than one job or overtime. She typically has a more difficult time acquiring strong partnerships and childcare, which is not always available, so she would require a babysitter, as well as seeking child support and living in a secure atmosphere because she is forced to do everything on her own.

A single mother can also defined as a woman who is widowed, divorced, or unmarried but receives financial support from the child's father, a significant other, or some succession. Divorced women who share legal custody with their male spouses are more likely to be eligible for child support or other forms of financial aid than other "single mothers". In well-functioning co-parenting scenarios, both mothers and fathers share parental and financial responsibilities for their children.

WHEN YOU WERE YOUNG, DID YOUR DAD ASSIST WITH NECESSARY BILLS?   

HAVE BOTH OF YOUR PARENTS BEEN PHYSICALLY PRESENT FOR YOU DURING PIVOTAL MOMENTS OF YOUR LIFE?   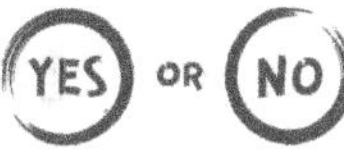

WOULD YOU CONSIDER YOURSELF A "SINGLE" MOTHER"?   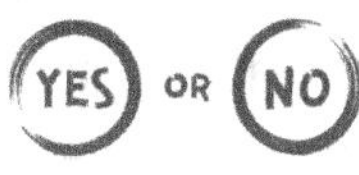

LIST 5 STRONG SINGLE MOTHERS YOU LOOK UP TOO:

The rising prevalence of single motherhood has led some women to start families without fully considering their personal growth, financial stability, or the advantages of a two-parent household. When children lack emotional support from their parents, they often experience increased anxiety and confusion. Deep down, every child longs for their parents to stay together, finding comfort in the stability and love of a united family —a desire that often persists well into adolescence.

Fathers play a vital role in providing a sense of security and stability for their children. When actively involved, they inspire both sons and daughters to strive for success, often motivated by the desire for their father's approval and love. If we bring children into the world without considering their long-term well-being beyond population growth, we risk failing the next generation.

DOMINOES

Many women, despite their love, dedication, and commitment to their families and communities, have been abandoned by those they trusted—even when their vulnerabilities were well-known. Mothers, in particular, face immense pressure to be flawless and to take on the responsibility of solving society's problems. With limited support and few alternatives, they often bear the full burden of raising, educating, and shaping their children.

While some may argue that women choose to be unhappy in relationships, most enter them with genuine optimism. However, societal expectations and emotional vulnerabilities can leave them susceptible to manipulation. When these dynamics persist, they often lead to increased stress and unhappiness, making it even harder for women to find fulfillment and support in their relationships.

PAWNS

Mothers who use children as a tool for control, manipulation, or entrapment often struggle to create a nurturing and supportive environment. In some cases, a woman may intentionally become pregnant within a love triangle to cause harm or gain leverage over others. As a result, many of these children experience lasting emotional trauma, stemming from parental absence or strained family dynamics, which can impact their well-being and development.

LOSE

Postpartum depression can linger for weeks, months, or even years after childbirth, particularly in women who experience significant stress during pregnancy. These intense emotions inevitably influence the children involved. When this ripple effect is compounded by emotionally scarred mothers and disengaged fathers, it can lead to a generation of unhappy children who often grow into troubled adults.

Many of us hold such deep love for our mothers that we shy away from confronting the difficult truths about how our upbringing has shaped us psychologically and physically. Instead of addressing these issues, we tend to minimize them, rationalize our parents' behavior, or sweep the past under the rug, pretending it never happened.

DO YOU HAVE ANY UNRESOLVED CHILDHOOD ISSUES? 

IS YOUR MOTHER SOMEONE YOU CAN OPEN UP TO ABOUT THE THINGS THAT ARE IMPORTANT TO YOU? 

WHAT'S YOUR VIEW? WHY?

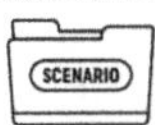

FEMALES OF SINGLE MOMMAS

The harsh reality is, that some of today's young ladies grew up in households with only one parent and credit their mothers for instilling the strength and independence to succeed. It's unfortunate when women who have experienced their fair share of tragedy teach their daughters that survival comes before love. They share their life experiences with their girls to help prevent them from making the same mistakes they made. This is done out of a desire to protect their daughters, but it also involves the projection of the mother's fears and pain onto the next generation of women, many of whom may have witnessed the hardships their mothers went through to provide for them.

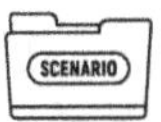

MALES WITH FATHERS ISSUES

Young men still look for ways to heal from the pain and anger they feel toward their biological fathers that they have harbored for a long time. Others have dedicated their entire life to dealing with inconsistent and absent actions. Even though many people have died without ever finding who their biological father was, the subject remains taboo in many families and has created generational curses.

We may all agree that both parents are to blame; but one of them must accept responsibility for their actions and acknowledge the need to be honest with their children, who will one day become dads themselves.

It is the responsibility of young women to ensure that the guy with whom they choose to have children is well-informed about himself and his family history so that he can provide appropriate names for his offspring.

Overall, some men are oblivious to the psychological harm they've caused to women's lives. As a result, they are quick to point the finger of blame at the mothers who instill in their daughters the values of independence and perseverance.

Notes:

TRICK OR TRICK?

Quote:
A mistake repeated more than once is a decision!

One of the worst and most harmful characteristics a person can possess is dishonesty because of its association with both bad home life and criminal activity. Never lie unless doing so is necessary to protect yourself or another person.

Oftentimes, a person's dishonest tendencies can be traced back to their early upbringing. They may have started off telling fibs now and then, but their dishonest behavior is far more consistent now than it was when they first started. This is why it's important to take action right away if you notice such behavior in children before it develops into a habit.

It should go without saying that I am not referring to situations where it is necessary to tell a lie or only reveal part of the truth to avoid endangering the lives of others. Most people are too polite to give their honest opinion when a close friend or family member asks for it on a personal or sensitive matter. Nonetheless, I think it's crucial to express one's thoughts and emotions openly and honestly, especially if doing so will help others. In the long run, people will respect your honesty.

Have you dated a pathological liar?

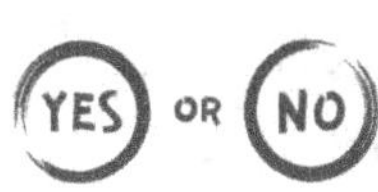

DISMISSED

I've witnessed employees and managers alike lying about their motivations when it comes to avoiding contact with customers. While even the most apparent lies are usually easy to discern, white lies are the most subtle kind of deception.

Appointment scheduling, supply shortages, and projected work hours are all examples of factors that could present challenges that aren't always easy to resolve. This presents a number of issues for businesses, including the potential for financial loss and the danger of alienating their clientele.

TRAITS

How many times have you caught someone you love in a lie? When it comes to being able to appreciate another person, people who lie compulsively are in a completely different category than the rest of us, and this is where issues start to arise. When someone tells a lie, they are putting their own needs and wants ahead of the needs of the people who are closest to them in their life.

This can have serious consequences. It is a widespread misconception that if a person tells a lie, it is because they care for the other person and don't want to risk losing them. This is not entirely the case, in the end, they are more concerned about how it will directly affect them if they are caught as opposed to how it will affect the situation as a whole.

Someone who suffers from pathological lying may be willing to put their own life in jeopardy to cover up their behavior. This includes the possibility of going away; to maintain you as a part of their life if it is advantageous, they are willing to take this risk.

Despite this, you may still be required to look into the potential that they staged their demise. A skilled storyteller, much like a con artist, may convince their audience that any lie can be believed by skillfully weaving it into an engaging narrative and making it sound convincing. They may have high levels of insecurity that they regard life as a competition, and because of their feelings of inadequacy, they are unable to appreciate genuine enjoyment in the accomplishments of others. Even when they are thrilled for you, they may try to downplay the significance of what you've accomplished to take credit for achievements they believe they deserve.

The vast majority of liars are so self-absorbed and careless, the possibility of them posing a threat to anyone whose life cross with theirs is exceedingly high. This is especially true for people whose lives involve romantic relationships. After you have moved on with your life, the person you are abandoning as a consequence of the circumstance may suffer feelings of rejection, indifference, or abandonment as a result of the situation. On the surface, they appear to be strong competitors, but that is not the reality.

Signs of jealousy or claiming credit for successes they think he deserves can be seen. Liars immediately identify their own guilt and will stretch the truth to excuse their acts, if you observe this behavior more than twice, you should have a serious conversation with the individual, issue a strong warning, or make plans to leave the situation, depending on how serious the problem is. Some lies are more extreme than others, ignoring the issue for an extended period of time will only make it worse and more common.

Lies have the capacity to completely change the direction of a person's life. It may be used as a coping mechanism by people with antisocial or narcissistic personality disorders who have experienced abuse or trauma. Many people have preconceived notions about pathological liars, such that they are crafty liars whose lying serves an ulterior motive. However, you have no business passing judgment on people for lying if you have difficulties telling the truth yourself. There is no right or wrong reason to lie, but if you can't seem to get along with others, maybe it's time to start with yourself.

Making tough choices is never simple, but it's necessary to fix what went wrong. Admitting one has a bad habit is the first step in changing it. Depending on the gravity of the situation, realizing you have a mental illness may prompt you to seek professional care immediately.

What lies have your partner(s) told you?

What was the reason the relationship ended?

YES OR NO

Be honest! Do you think of yourself as someone who lies or deceives? 

How often do you lie or deceive for your personal benefit?

1   **2**   **3**   **4**   **5**

RARELY   AVERAGE   FREQUENTLY

What are the main reasons for your dishonesty?

What are you doing or plan to do, to change your habit?

WHAT MEN REALLY WANT!?

"You always want what you can't have" - Sherry Argov

Before addressing the gender gap, it's important to understand how men and women often see the world differently. This can shape their desires and expectations, particularly in relationships. Through discussions, I often gain new insights into the male perspective. Men frequently express the feeling that women are indifferent to their needs, even at the most basic level. Despite individual differences, many men maintain a consistent outlook, regardless of their background or experiences.

It's widely acknowledged that men's expectations of a partner vary. For example, some women believe that "broken men seek women to heal them; immature men look for a mother figure; mature men desire an equal partner; hardworking men want support; and lazy men seek enablers." This perspective may not be universally true, but it resonates with the experiences of many.

Understanding that men and women are driven by different motives is key to navigating relationships. These differences shouldn't lead one partner to accuse the other of selfishness, as both can exhibit self-centered behavior at times. The real tension arises when one person feels they are giving more than they receive. Complacency, which can develop from the routine and ease of daily life, often exacerbates these issues. To foster healthier relationships, recognizing and addressing these dynamics is essential.

PRIVACY

As social media has grown in popularity, it has become increasingly difficult to keep private or sacred information safe in today's environment. Everything is exposed for everyone to view and learn about, which raises the bar for many expectations. Now more than ever, there are options available to satisfy the leisure needs of singles, making it more pleasurable for those without romantic partners to live independently.

To put it plainly, it appears that modern men and women no longer feel they need each other for the reasons their parents taught them or for the reasons they have historically been expected to. More and more, it appears that people don't care how they get happiness in their relationships; instead, they'd rather just be happy, period.

This may make it harder for single people who happen to cross paths frequently to develop love feelings for one another and get married. Factors such as family, friends, social media, ego, feminism, and money can either foster or hinder a couple's ability to develop their relationship. Successful dating in the modern era favors women who put in the time and effort to learn about men and the things that motivate them.

SEX & INTIMACY

Regardless of their relationship status, many men often find themselves daydreaming about attractive women they encounter. A common challenge for them is their curiosity and desire to learn more about women from different backgrounds. If we accept the traditional narrative of Adam and Eve, it suggests that men have historically been more easily captivated by women.

A man's sincerity can be questioned if, upon first meeting you, he claims to value your achievements and independence more than your appearance, sexual appeal, or judgment. However, over time and through closer observation, a person's true nature will eventually become evident.

In the dating world, men should focus on finding a woman who is interested in engaging in conversation and going on dates. The way these conversations unfold often shapes the rest of their time together, whether it's during the day or night.

When it comes to attraction, a man's priority is likely to include a desire for intimacy with a woman—not only immediately but also throughout their interaction. While men's sexual desires parallel a woman's need for love and affection, both can lead to complications. In the early stages of dating, a man might not envision a future involving love, marriage, or children—and he may still feel uncertain about those possibilities even after several months.

Moreover, the dynamics of attraction can be further complicated by societal expectations and personal experiences. Many men grapple with the pressures to conform to masculine ideals and may feel conflicted about expressing vulnerability or deep emotional connections. This can result in a hesitancy to fully engage in relationships, prioritizing physical interaction over emotional investment. As they navigate these complexities, men may find that understanding their own motivations and desires, as well as those of the women they're interested in, is crucial for fostering genuine connections that transcend superficial attraction.

Ultimately, effective communication and mutual respect can pave the way for more meaningful relationships, allowing both partners to explore their feelings and intentions comfortably.

Be realistic and wary as you weigh a man's statements and actions. As a result of sexual interactions, many women make the mistake of allowing themselves to become emotionally attached or pregnant. Both words and sexual activity do not ensure a relationship. A man's emotional reaction to you and his subsequent choice needs time to develop. While waiting, try to draw attention to yourself for something more interesting and remarkable than your sex life. If you want to connect with the boys of today, you need to put reason and common sense ahead of your feelings.

A man's deeds can sometimes contradict his words. Men are inherently particular, which is why this is the case. Some men will say to a lady exactly what they think she wants to hear.

SPACE

Men have traditionally been more guarded about their personal space than women, which is often why many guys seek out their own private retreats within the home, commonly known as a "man cave." This designated area allows them to unwind after a busy day, offering a sanctuary for activities like watching TV, playing video games, or simply enjoying a few moments of peace and quiet. It's essential to recognize that a man who values this alone time is deserving of a woman's admiration, as it reflects his need for personal space to recharge and cultivate his interests.

Furthermore, it's important for women to understand and respect this aspect of a man's personality. By doing so, she can foster a supportive atmosphere within the relationship. Teaching children to accept and appreciate their father's need for solitude can also contribute to a healthy family dynamic. A diligent worker and responsible adult should have the space to relax without feeling guilty or pressured to constantly engage. This respect for personal boundaries not only strengthens the marital bond but also sets a positive example for children, illustrating the importance of self-care and the value of personal time for everyone, regardless of gender. In cultivating an environment where personal space is honored, both partners can thrive individually and together.

Keep in mind, he is free to leave if he can't relax in this environment. Why wouldn't you want the breadwinner to feel comfortable and safe at home?

Men enjoy being with other men for the same reason they want a man cave—space to unwind. However, they also seek places to relax without constant reminders of bills and responsibilities, as a man cave can feel isolating. Men and women are wired differently, so approaching this from a female perspective can miss the mark. Many women believe their partners should spend free time helping with chores and kids, but men may view "free time" differently.

Regardless of cultural norms, it's important to discuss expectations before starting a family. Many working fathers are exhausted after a long day and prefer to relax rather than help with homework. While you and your partner may not always agree, learning to compromise strengthens the relationship.

Women who understand this often take on more domestic roles, especially those involving children. When one side frequently wishes they were somewhere else, there is a good chance that there are problems. It's respectful to try to figure things out with your partner, whether you're married or not. Despite appearances, one should never give up hope, because every relationship has the potential to be mutually beneficial.

LOGIC & UNDERSTANDING

Perhaps men don't always talk about how they feel, but when they do, women may want to hear them out. It should be a woman's concerns if she is in a relationship in which she is uncertain of her partner's mental frame of mind or current emotions. Men will show you things they like or want, drop hints, tell jokes, and chat a lot if they think you're paying attention, but they'll stop communicating altogether if they think you're not. Men tend to internalize their thoughts and feelings, with much of their thoughts revolving around matters of monetary and professional variety. Despite their outward demeanor, tend to be harsh critics of themselves. They can be unduly critical of themselves and the way they handle the obligations of daily life at times, particularly as they become older and begin to feel as though they are not making sufficient progress.

You may be met with hostility or ignored altogether, so don't be startled if you don't hear back from someone after bringing up an issue. Don't let things go that bad, even though it seems immature that men don't always show their feelings the way women do. He will start giving you the answers you want to hear if you keep asking the same questions.

Remember that silence can sometimes transmit a great deal of information, but don't be afraid to ask and say what you need to when he is in the mood for a serious chat. It's easy to accept a man's behavior, so it's important to always use logic and common sense and never let yourself get delusional about the conditions. Even if certain things don't become perfectly clear right away, rest assured that you'll have all you need to decide how to move on wisely.

CONCLUSION

In conclusion, I have come to the opinion that there is a considerable gap between the actual needs that men have and the wants that they articulate. It's unclear if males will ever be content, but it seems they'll never stop searching for short-term satisfaction. They may settle with whatever temporarily satisfies their emotional needs. It's up to the woman to figure out whether her man wants a little solitude or a little romance.

Women need to learn to have a life outside of their relationships so they may learn to channel their emotions into meaningful goals and aspirations. As someone who is perpetually preoccupied with her ambitions, I can attest to the need to respect the personal space of a significant other.

While satisfying their physical needs is important, men's primary desires lie in the periodic need for praise and recognition. Men can be fussy when it comes to having sex, thus they require a lady who is both submissive and dominant. Maintaining a pleasant aroma at all times. Modern men place a premium on having financial security, a supportive partner, and a personality that resembles that of their mother.

They're on the lookout for a well-balanced friend for life. One of the most important needs is to be treated with respect, even if they don't deserve it.

What do you agree with?

What do you disagree with?

Do you feel that most men know what they want? YES OR NO

Does your partner express himself when an issue arises? YES OR NO

Do you feel modern men are jealous of modern independent women? YES OR NO

Are women today more aggressive than before? YES OR NO

What are your experiences?

TRADITIONAL VALUES IN A CONTEMPORARY WORLD

Quote:

"Our modern society is engaged in polishing and decorating the cage in which man is kept imprisoned." - Nirmalananda

GAP

Over the years, the discrepancy between what we were taught, and reality has grown significantly. Men who grew up in the 1970s and 1980s and had at least one male role model in their lives—their father, grandpa, or uncle—were more likely to absorb the idea that men should be the breadwinners and the head of the household. They also instilled in them the importance of working hard and striving for big things; inspired by the great men in their family, each member did what he could to follow in their footsteps.

Men in today's culture are under a lot of pressure to excel and prove themselves in every aspect of their life. This unease may be traced back to several factors, including the advent of today's modern women, the unpredictable state of the economy, and the rapid growth of technology.

As modern women have evolved, men have become more defensive, competitive, and dissatisfied in romantic relationships.

Do you agree?   (YES) OR (NO)   *Other:* ___________

MODERN CONFLICT

Even today's progressive women have accepted the new paradigm. Most of the modern concepts of women's independence and self-sufficiency were passed down from mothers to their daughters. Inconsistent gender roles lead to unequal expectations, which is cause for concern. These days' ladies know they can get a lot done even without a man at their side. They are thriving professionally, providing for their households, and bringing up their children with little help from outsiders.

It's encouraging to see individuals acquiring autonomy and confidence, but it's troubling to see them having children in which their connections are hazy at best. The ideas and standards that have historically been linked with men's perspectives are, in the eyes of many modern women, difficult and unneeded. These women have been socialized to feel that they must abandon these traits because they are outdated. In general, women who say things like "I don't need a man" are showing signs of growing independence and a preference for taking charge of their own lives and making their own decisions. These women probably don't represent the archetype of conventional femininity, which prioritizes submission, housework, and formality.

After so much progress has been accomplished by women, average men may be left wondering how they fit into a world dominated by successful women. Whether or not they stayed at home to raise their children, our faithful grandparents always made sure we had hot meals and a tidy place to live.

Any modern male who wants to start a conversation with a modern woman needs to quickly understand the idea that today's strong, independent women were raised by an entirely different generation of women.

Women shouldn't assume that all men see the world the same way they do in terms of the dynamic reshaping of gender roles and views of men. Men, however, were taught how to interact with traditional feminine ideas when they were brought up still believing in traditional values.

WHAT TRADITIONAL GENDER ROLES WOULD YOU INCLUDE IN YOUR RELATIONSHIP AND HOUSEHOLD?

MOMMAS AND THEIR BOYS!

"A man loves his sweetheart the most, his wife the best, but his mother the longest." — Irish Proverb

NO SECRET

There is this widely held belief that the connection between a man and his mother is supernatural. As a consequence of this theory, we wish that Momma would have told us that they bear the responsibility for producing the "Mama's boys" of the world. It's commonly known that today's boys and men are brought up in a very different environment than their counterparts of twenty or thirty years ago. While this amazing connection has allowed for a great deal of in-depth engagement, it has also put a strain on many partnerships, including marriages.

Wives and girlfriends of "mama's boys" may mistakenly believe that they are competing with the man's mother for his attention. The truth is that she is fighting an uphill struggle against the man's mother. Most boys treat their mothers with undying devotion and respect because doing so is a sacred duty in their society. They do this as a token of their gratitude for all the ways their mothers have helped them grow and succeed.

With these tensions, many guys have a difficult time finding partners and maintaining them since the women they date may occasionally find their behavior with their mothers odd and unfavorable. This makes it difficult for the males to maintain relationships.

CONFLICT OF INTEREST

Conflict inside the family may generate the appearance that they are competing with the "other woman," especially if jealousy plays a role on both sides of the argument. It is common for a man's mother and his partner, the two most significant women in his life, to compete with one another for his unwavering loyalty. This is typical of a man who values his family highly and is prepared to put in days and nights to provide for everyone. However, if grandkids are present, it's important to remember that the heated discussion could have an impact on them as well.

The son's development will likely suffer as a result of the family's frequent conflicts. If the son continues to react with passive-aggressive behavior after the fundamental problems have been brushed under the rug and life has been restored to an acceptable condition, it may be because he is still processing the trauma he experienced. One way to achieve this goal is to pretend that nothing is wrong, to take opposing viewpoints, or to simply ignore the problem. The lack of genuine communication between the warring parties may be taken as an indication of his disinterest or weakness if he provides that impression.

Therefore, he is going through an emotional roller coaster, and he closes down as a result of the strain, stress, or negative energy he feels. For the sake of a happy life and future, "Mama's boys" would do their best to work through this issue as soon as possible.

TABLES DO TURN

Mothers of sons, wives, and girlfriends will have an in-depth understanding of vengeance and mutual respect after starting their own families. They are more likely to agree to tone down the bickering and be courteous with each other if the grandparents notice that their grandkids are having a hard time as a result of the situation. Because grandmothers love their grandkids so much, they often look for ways to spend as much time as possible with them. A mother should never, ever, ever utilize the bond her children share with their grandparents as bargaining leverage in a conflict with the other party.

In no uncertain terms is this acceptable behavior. Many husbands, upon witnessing such behavior on the side of their spouses, either feel animosity or attempt to rationalize it. Both of these options should be avoided at all costs because neither is desirable nor is it suitable. As a culture, we have allowed some aspects of tradition to be used as an excuse to forgive undesirable conduct demonstrated by moms for far too long.

This has been a problem. If a son is typically the sole provider for his mother, he may establish unhealthy routines with his mother that are difficult to overcome. Nonetheless, the son is the only one who can resolve the current issues by first acknowledging that there is a problem and then seeking a solution that both women can agree on. This is because the son values the opinions of both women and wants to keep the peace and harmony, they have worked so hard to achieve. It is essential for them to put their differences aside and work toward mending their relationship with one another as this will allow them to move forward.

All adults have a duty to put in this effort for the sake of maintaining the vitality of the connections they have with one another. The pursuit of drama is a fruitless endeavor that will inevitably end in unhappiness for the individuals involved in it.

HOW TO SPOT THEM

There are some adult males who, despite having the financial resources necessary to support themselves independently, continue to spend a significant amount of time with their parents or even live with them. This is the case even though they are financially capable of living on their own. Even after they have moved out on their own, some sons continue to maintain a close relationship with their mothers by paying them daily visits, running errands, shopping for groceries, and in some cases even paying the bills when it is absolutely necessary to do so.

This is especially (though not exclusively) true for mothers who are raising their children by themselves, whether as the result of a divorce or as a result of difficulties they may be having with their health. In the vast majority of instances, this does not present a problem until it does.

CHARACTERISTICS

When a man is brought up exclusively by his mother, it is only natural for him to take on some of her characteristics and ways of thinking, at least to some extent. It's possible that these guys have traits such as egotism, dependence, emotion, sensitivity, protectiveness, and even some traditionally feminine traits.

Many men raised without a father figure struggle with unresolved emotional issues, making it difficult for them to express love and support for others. There are such things as generational curses, and how a man's parents brought them up, in addition to their environment, may have long-term consequences.

I've seen exceptions to this rule time and time again in the form of men who grew up without a father figure but turned out to be wonderful fathers and husbands. This indicates that regardless of one's shortcomings, it is entirely up to an individual to resolve to be better and commit to avoiding repeating previous cycles, irrespective of his circumstances.

DECISIONS

Ancestry research is more significant now than it has ever been before because a person's parents and grandparents are the building blocks upon which their family history is constructed. Not only will learning about the past of your prospective partner provide you with knowledge for enlightenment, but it will also prepare you for unexpected circumstances that might arise in the future. It is not for the sole purpose of passing a harsh judgment or eliminating someone from consideration.

No one will give you an unvarnished account of reality, and even those who do may only give you the parts they think you want to hear. However, in the end, it is up to the individual to decide whether or not they feel safe enough to discuss their personal life with you. It is your responsibility to determine whether or you feel sufficiently secure with your personal decisions.

You owe it to yourself to evaluate your level of preparedness to deal with whatever it is you're considering taking on. If not, there is always someone else who can help, but they should not feel forced to keep those issues to themselves or share them if they are not ready to do so.

If a man has recently lost his mother, either through her passing or her abandonment, he needs to take time for himself and reflect privately and in silence on the meaning of this loss. When a man loses his mother, he may feel an emptiness inside of himself that can never be filled by anything or anyone else, no matter how much they try. Some men may react hostilely, emotionally distance themselves, or with apathy, all of which will make the situation more complicated. Others self-medicate with drugs, alcohol, or other vices to dull the pain of their loss, while others lean more heavily than ever before on their significant other or the company of others.

There is no substitute for professional counseling when it comes to coping with grief; however, you can help someone else get through the loss of a loved one more quickly by allowing them the space and time to mourn on their terms and by expressing empathy and patience for their loss.

BATTLE WON

It is in your best interest to avoid getting into an argument with a man's mother because you are the only person, he will never forgive for disrespecting her. If you want your relationship with the family of your spouse to be truly enjoyable and fulfilling, you must always show respect to your in-laws, even if you do not believe that respect is warranted.

Many of us enter into new romantic partnerships with the optimistic expectation that we can alter at least the partner's personality or the partnership's dynamic. This is due to our confidence in our ability to influence or in some cases manipulate the other individual. However, these situations almost never go as planned.

Realize that the link between a man and his mother did not form over the course of a single night and that nothing can be done to sever it. If it does happen, it won't derail your plans and probably even work out for the better. If a man is having issues with his mom, it's important to avoid becoming frustrated or overly involved in the situation. Instead, consider finding alternative activities to do with him. However, there may be instances where it is appropriate to offer your thoughts and suggestions, as long as they are carefully considered and respectful.

Sometimes, women tend to take the side of their partners without considering the other perspective. By doing so, you can demonstrate to your spouse that you are striving to alleviate their stress, and you may even establish a newfound bond with their mother. Showing your partner that you are making an effort to ease their struggles is a strong display of your gratitude towards them. It's crucial to maintain a positive attitude and take productive steps, despite any obstacles in your way. This will illustrate your dedication to your partner and your relationship.

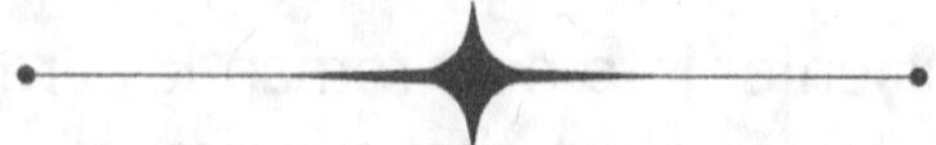

DESCRIBE YOUR RELATIONSHIP WITH YOUR SIGNIFICANT OTHER'S MOTHER OR MOTHER FIGURE IN FOUR (4) WORDS.

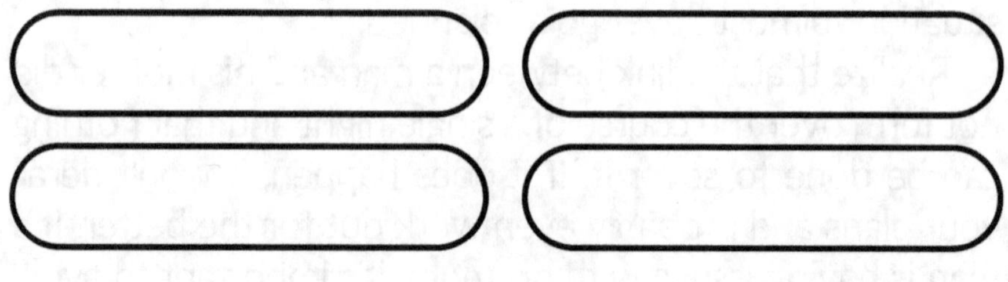

Have you dated a "Momma's Boy" 

Are you a mother of a son? 

MOMMY ISSUES

It's possible for boys and men of all ages to experience "mommy issues" if they have a strained or unpleasant relationship with their mothers. This can occur due to a lack of affection, such as in the case of an emotionally distant mother, or an excess of love, such as in an environment with no boundaries. While mothers and sons share a unique bond, there are occasions when their interactions can be painful or hurtful for both parties. From infancy, some mothers may be overprotective and want to shield their children from the world's potential dangers. Young males who lack confidence and stability during their formative years may be more prone to becoming socially awkward and dependent adults.

When in a committed relationship, it's natural to have concerns about how someone behaves around other women. Sudden shifts in affection could suggest a need for validation or social insecurity. It's also understandable to feel hesitant or unsure about fully committing to a partner. Seeking your parents' approval before making big decisions is normal, but it can be difficult if you have trouble communicating or spending time with your mother.

To make informed decisions about how to address certain issues, it's important to recognize the characteristics of men who experience them. When dealing with such situations, it's crucial to be patient and empathetic, understanding that these individuals may have had little control over their upbringing.

Offering words of reassurance can be extremely helpful if your significant other is struggling with self-doubt or could use some inspiration. However, it's important not to judge them too quickly if they're in a precarious situation. While you may not be able to change the dynamics of some relationships, there are still various ways you can try to help and hopefully improve the situation for everyone involved.

Do you think that men are to blame for the way in which their moms treat the women they've chosen? 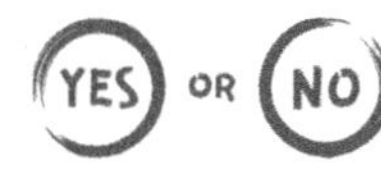

Is this type of guy a deal breaker? 

Are you dealing with someone with "Mommy issues"?

- ○ Criticism of self as well as others
- ○ Impulsive lifestyle
- ○ Commitment issue in relationships
- ○ Low Self-esteem
- ○ Poor social interactions
- ○ Envy and jealousy of others' success
- ○ Compares women to his mother
- ○ Unable to handle criticism
- ○ Codependent
- ○ Lacks boundaries dealing with people
- ○ Lacks accountability in situations
- ○ Clingy

Have you dated a man with "mommy issues"?   (YES) OR (NO)

How did you address the issues?

____

____

____

____

Notes:

Notes:

CASE OF THE EX!

""Pain makes you stronger, fear makes you braver, heartbreak makes you wiser."" — Unknown

CYCLE

Even the most painful breakups can turn out to be beneficial in the long run, but we won't sugarcoat the exes we wish we could forget. However, everyone has a past love who remains in their thoughts and memories.

It's possible for a relationship to terminate in one of three ways, and each of them is laden with negativity: amicably, toxically, or conditionally. Many people have trouble moving on after a relationship ends because they never felt like the relationship was resolved or that they had emotionally recovered from the pain of the split. It seems like exes always want to find someone else to blame for the breakup of their relationship.

More often than not, new romantic partnerships prove to be futile for the majority of the people that try them. Most people, when their romantic relationships finish, jump right into another one in an effort to find happiness again as soon as possible. When two people who aren't emotionally compatible begin a relationship, the other person will eventually take advantage of the victim's naivete and paint them as the bad guy. It's a vicious cycle all over again!

For someone starting over this journey has been greatly aided by people who have grown and developed through introspection and self-healing. Some of them had been alone for quite some time by this point because they waited to start a relationship until they were completely prepared.

EX FACTOR

Exes have the power to evoke a wide range of feelings in their exes. Those who already have a personal, tangible investment in causing trouble for another person should be avoided at all costs. Those who are unable to move on from their past relationships have an emotional connection to their exes even though they are no longer in a physical relationship with them. In the face of feelings where loved ones have been severed by death, betrayal, deep hurt, or regret, one may feel trapped in a mental prison from which there is no escape.

People that live in the past may give the impression of being in love relationships to those who don't know any better. When it comes to more in-depth conversations or prospects for advancement, they may become frustrated or busy with other concerns. If you are able to recognize the signs, not only will you be able to avoid getting hurt, but you will also save yourself wasted time.

WEB

It's simple to become entangled in a pit of lies, doubt, and anger concerning an EX. Humans frequently exhibit what psychologists call the "see-saw effect," in which they swing back and forth emotionally before finally withdrawing from a person or situation.

Sadly, many people unwittingly succumb to the emotional, physical, and psychological repercussions related to a former loved one. It's normal to feel sad and worried if you've drifted apart from a loved one after putting in a lot of effort to stay in touch. However, if you intend to involve someone unaware of your feelings toward your ex-partner, you should exercise caution and consideration. Reuniting with an ex-spouse and achieving everlasting happiness is uncommon.

Divorce is often the result of unresolved emotional or physical problems, and unmet expectations, which can have lasting effects on individuals. It's crucial to address the root causes of past tension to prevent similar problems from arising in future relationships. It's important to keep in mind that single exes were previously in a relationship that ended for a variety of reasons. Rushing into a new relationship without first understanding the full story and expecting emotional baggage to disappear overnight can harm both individuals involved.

REBOUND

When someone jumps into a new serious relationship right after ending a previous one without taking enough time to heal emotionally, it is called a "rebound relationship". This can occur due to physical distance or death, but in my opinion, grieving after a loss often takes longer and may require professional help. It is often observed that individuals struggle to handle the various distressing emotions that may arise after the termination of a romantic relationship due to their inadequate coping mechanisms.

Certain individuals tend to carry their past issues into their current relationships, hindering their progress. Despite being aware of the reasons behind a couple's separation, one cannot disregard the reality of the situation. Relationships may fail for various reasons, as feelings can change over time and people sometimes act impulsively when they're frustrated or upset. Experts recommend taking a break before making any major changes, to give any unresolved issues a chance to surface. It's common for people to unwittingly become a rebound for someone else at some point in their lives.

It's common for some individuals to seek solace in a new relationship after a breakup, particularly if their previous partner has already moved on. While it would be ideal for everyone to weigh the consequences of their actions beforehand, many individuals make the mistake of diving into a rebound relationship and then become surprised when it doesn't work out. However, it's important to note that although they may not have initially entered the relationship with full commitment, they have the capacity to change over time. Loving and committing to each other are choices that can be made.

DO YOU FEEL REGRET AFTER RECONCILING WITH AN EX? 

HAVE YOU EVER FOUND YOURSELF IN A RELATIONSHIP WHERE THE OTHER PERSON WAS STILL EMOTIONALLY ATTACHED TO THEIR EX? 

HAVE YOU EVER USED SOMEONE AS A REBOUND? 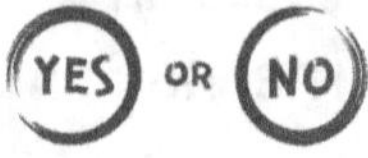

PREY

It is not uncommon for individuals to unintentionally find themselves in a rebound relationship or actively seek out a rebounder. "Rebounders" are usually sincere individuals who believe their partner when they claim to be emotionally ready for a new romantic relationship after their previous one. The person pursuing the rebound will often choose a partner who makes them feel like they have advanced or improved their love life, whether it's through physical attraction, social status, lifestyle, or sexual intimacy.

Although the longevity of a rebound relationship can be surprising, it usually mirrors the healing process of both individuals involved. Unfortunately, it may take years for the victim of a rebound relationship to realize they were part of this dynamic.

DOES THE PREVIOUS RELATIONSHIP HISTORY OF A DATE MATTER?  

DO YOU THINK IT TAKES MOST PEOPLE 1-2 YEARS TO FULLY RECOVER FROM PAST RELATIONSHIPS? 

DO YOU HAVE AN EX THAT YOU'RE HAVING A HARD TIME MOVING ON FROM? 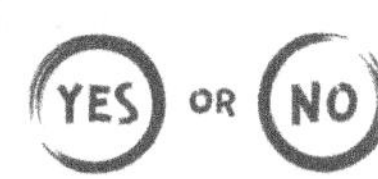

If you have selected more than TWO of the following red flags, it may indicate that your current relationship is a rebound:

☐ COMPARING CURRENT PARTNER TO AN EX.

☐ SPEAKING ABOUT THE EX-CONSTANTLY WHETHER NEGATIVE OR POSITIVELY.

☐ COMMITMENT ISSUES, NO PROGRESSION! EXAMPLE: MARRIAGE, RELOCATION ETC.

☐ SECRETLY COMMUNICATING WITH EXES.

☐ MIRRORING OR COMPETING WITH EX'S LIFE.

☐ AVOIDING INTRODUCTION TO FAMILY AND FRIENDS.

☐ INABILITY TO CONNECT WITH YOUR PARTNER ON A DEEP LEVEL.

☐ KEEPING MEMENTOS OUT OF NOSTALGIA FOR THE PAST. IMAGES, JEWELRY, AND MEMENTOS

☐ KEEPING UP WITH THEIR SOCIAL MEDIA, REACTING TO POSTS & PICTURES.

☐ JUST RECENTLY ENDED A LONG-TERM COMMITMENT MARRIAGE, DIVORCE, CO-PARENTING, ETC.

Do you have a good understanding of your partner's past? Knowing their patterns can provide insight into their personality.

The following could also be used as a guide while you navigate the dating world.

- How did your significant other and his ex meet?

- How long did their previous relationship last?

- Before dating, how long did they break up?

- Why did they break up?

- Does your partner still have love for his ex?

- What were regrets from his previous relationship?

- When was the last time your partner and his ex were intimate?

- How serious was your partner's relationship with his ex?

- Is your partner still in contact with ex-partners?

- Do they keep in touch on social media?

- Did your partner introduce his ex's parents to him?

- Are ex-partners still in contact with your partner's family?

- Are they convicted felons?

- Have you checked the sex offender registry?

- What is your partner's educational background?

- What is the professional background of your partner?

- What is the credit score of your partner?

- What are their religious or spiritual beliefs?

- Your partner's thoughts on global social and economic issues?

Notes:

DUST YOUR SHOULDERS OFF!

Quote:
"Not all storms come to disrupt your life. Some come to clear your path." — Paulo Coelho

BAD

Tragedies, interpersonal conflicts, and strained relationships all bring out the worst in people, and everyone has seen their loved ones at their worst. This holds true regardless of the nature of the conflict. When someone close to you puts your happiness in peril for no apparent reason, it's tough to fathom their motivations.

Everyone eventually displays their true colors and intents, and as you gain wisdom and experience, you will be able to spot red flags at an earlier stage in the process. We won't always be able to avoid difficulties, but being prepared will help us face them with more strength and resolve.

Even if you're already in a great relationship with someone who seems to be everything you've been looking for on the surface—someone who is compassionate, supportive, and everything you've been looking for in a partner—it is easy to have your preconceived assumptions about your existing spouse destroyed by news or an unexpected encounter.

BLAME GAME

Even though you recognize your humanity now, in the past you may have been the "other woman" who knowingly chose to ruin a family or a relationship. No matter how you feel about the morality of adultery, it is obvious that all parties involved may be dealing with someone who is dishonest, unscrupulous, and inconsiderate to the parties involved well-being. Whether or not you think adultery is wrong, it's obvious that everyone in the above situation is being exploited and someone always gets hurt in the end. While it may provide short-term pleasure and sexual excitement, someone will inevitably suffer as a result.

Some might justify their actions by claiming that only married individuals engage in adultery and other forms of infidelity. If your actions are in line with your own reading of the Scriptures or your rationalization of what you feel is just or acceptable, exploiting another person is still unethical. Given that we all have a moral compass—a conscience—we can instantly recognize when we're about to engage in behavior that is unethical or improper. No matter how much you try to deny it, it will always be the case.

Despite the widespread belief that men are more inclined to cheat than women, the responsibility for such actions may sometimes fall on both spouses. Many people, especially males, struggle to control their morality while they're flirting with a lady, they have strong feelings for. As a woman, it is your duty to ensure that the man you are interested in is not already attached to someone else at each level of his interest in you, this is usually the homework we as women fail to do.

DAMAGED

Experiencing the emotional and physical impacts of receiving bad news about a loved one from a stranger via phone, online, or in person is almost as distressing as hearing the news itself. Hiding something from your partner when you know they might find out is an act of selfishness. Those who have had their confidence betrayed may be especially susceptible to the negative psychological effects of the circumstance. Infidelity affects children, although most adults dealing with it don't give that much thought.

Some people may opt to isolate themselves after experiencing the emotional pain of an affair, which can last for quite some time. Even if your lover has been found cheating, it does not change the fact that you still love them, as everyone handles the emotional fallout of adultery differently. The reasons some people return to their partners after cheating or remain in miserable marriages are baffling to those on the outside looking in. It's important to keep in mind that there are times when many people have nowhere safe to go.

They may be compelled to live with their abuser in the marital home. On the day they get married, hardly one ever gives serious thought to the possibility of cheating on their spouse. Anxiety, low self-esteem, and being in a destructive relationship all contribute to the likelihood of cheating. Making the healthiest choice for oneself, one's kids, and one's family is the best approach to recovering from emotional stress.

INVESTIGATION

We've all been injured by someone we care about, trusted, and gave the benefit of the doubt, and it's not easy to get over that. Avoid dating someone who has recently ended a long-term relationship, especially if it was toxic or if the person, they trusted the most hurt their feelings, as anger and vengeance can surface quickly in such situations. The phrase "Hurt people, hurt people" is overstated, yet it is true. Expecting an injured person to love consistently and sincerely is like expecting a car with issues to run flawlessly.

Don't let your paranoia keep you from staying one step ahead of the competition. Before assuming the worst, look for clues and seek clarity. Instead of waiting months or years for an explanation and resolution of circumstances, do your homework and make the necessary improvements.

DETACHED

When we examine the personal and emotional connections that people have had throughout history, we see that there have been a large number of them. If our current love partner cannot deliver the intimacy we seek, we might look for another. These unexpected contacts have far-reaching impacts on society because people have a compulsive desire for continuing fulfillment through emotional and sexual behaviors.

This trend is undermining marriage and other forms of committed interpersonal relationships. It would be unfair to pin all of the responsibility on one sex group when both sexes' actions contributed to the problem's growth. Nothing will change, though, unless each of us attempts to change our behavior.

You can never find the joy and contentment in this life that you want if you refuse to recognize others for who they truly are. This isn't meant to justify or condone unethical conduct, but rather to provide light on why it occurs so often in committed partnerships. Keep an open mind and educate yourself on the motivations and thought processes of others if you want to find the person with whom you can spend the rest of your life and who will really love you. Then, and only then, will you meet the one person with whom you will share your life and who will love you unconditionally.

There is a lot of trial and error in love, just as there is in life. When it comes to managing relationships, people seldom choose a strategy that can be used in every circumstance. The true test is whether you can accept whatever difficulties you encounter with dignity and peace of mind. It's only you who can figure this out.

Have you ever lied or deceived someone in a relationship?

How many times?

Have you ever been cheated on?

How many times?

THE RUSH

One's urge to settle down with a spouse and start a family appears to increase as one approaches the age of thirty. Choosing between settling down and pursuing other goals is a common challenge in modern life, complicated by societal and familial pressures. It is commonly accepted that this change occurs sometime between a woman's late twenties and her forties. This pressure sometimes causes many ladies to have kids with guys who aren't emotionally, mentally, or monetarily ready to be dads.

If a guy thinks the woman conceived for financial or other material gain, he may decide to forsake the pregnancy and the child. As a general rule, men don't actively seek out sexual partners to become a parent, and women tend to have a deeper understanding of their bodies than men do. Therefore, in my opinion, a woman has complete control over her own body since she has the right to decide for herself whether or not she wants to have children. However, prioritizing one's own emotions over a child's welfare is an act of selfishness. A man's actions will reflect his feelings toward having children.

THE CLOCK

The term "biological clock" is often used to refer to a woman's fertile period and the time frame in which she has the greatest chance of becoming pregnant. While a woman is born with a certain number and quality of eggs, these characteristics gradually deteriorate as she ages.

This can make it more difficult for a woman to conceive as she gets older. Keep in mind that a woman's fertility can be affected by many factors and that every woman's experience of pregnancy and childbirth is unique.

The best course of action is not to rush in this situation. Avoid the mental anguish of maltreatment, broken homes, and financial struggles by giving yourself and your child the best possible start in life. If you are pushed for time, you have two options: either express to your significant other your thoughts and feelings about becoming a mother, as it is not erroneous for you to feel this way; or explain to your child how you feel about being a mother, since it is not inaccurate for you to feel this way. So that you and he are both on the same page, it's important to have this conversation right away.

If you and your partner are unable to make a decision that will satisfy both of you, it may be time to part ways and look for others who share your goals. Never trust a man who brazenly makes promises regarding your future if his behavior belies his words. He also shouldn't be pushed or coerced into starting a family before he's ready. Many people have struggled with this issue at some point in their lives; don't let yourself become a statistic.

Have you moved on from the person who caused you the greatest pain and forgiven them?

How many relationships have you been in?

What was your longest relationship?

When you think back on your past relationships, what factors led you to cheat on your spouse or significant other?

When you look back on your past relationships, what do you believe were the primary reasons your partner cheated on you, whether it was with another person or with you?

What advice would you provide to someone reeling from the grief of another person's infidelity?

SITUATIONSHIPS

"Oh, what a tangled web we weave, when first we practice to deceive!" -Sir Walter Scott

WHAT IS A SITUATIONSHIP?

Believe it or not, these ships have been sailing for years; the problem is that their parameters were never clearly specified, so the navigation may be a bit difficult to comprehend. Those who have sailed the chartered seas can attest that the waves can be rough depending on the weather conditions.

You may be scratching your head and asking, "What precisely do I mean, and what exactly is a situationship?"

A situational relationship, in contrast to a friendship or a love partnership, is more like ordering a combination meal than it is to have a platonic or romantic connection with someone you are fond of and like spending time with. There are strong emotional connections, but no clearly defined long-term goals; yet there is always the possibility of reaching a compromise.

It seems to me that a lot of people aren't content with the way traditional relationships are currently structured and the rules that come with them, some people prefer and they'd rather devote their time and energy to figuring out how to create and maintain a unique connection with another person on their terms, free from the heavy burdens and expectations that are typically associated with traditional romantic partnerships.

PHENOMENON

I was interested in the dynamics of human thought and interaction; therefore, I used a poll to learn how boredom and familiarity affect relationships. I like the use of polling to determine the level of interest in this topic among the general public. While it's true that many of these people may already be in stable relationships, the vast majority are also keen to meet new people and broaden their social horizons. Despite the persisting popularity of the swinging lifestyle, long-term commitment to a swinging partner is uncommon due to jealousy and other intense emotions.

One of the many things I have doubts about is whether or not humans are capable of experiencing true happiness. To be honest, I'm not sure they can. They may also be in search of novel methods to let go and have a good time. The rising divorce rate and negative media representations of marriage have contributed to widespread stigmatization of the institution. It seems that no one ever wishes to reach an age when they feel more restricted, especially in terms of acting in any way they please. Unfortunately, this holds regardless of the feelings of others.

Dating on the side is entertaining for a while, but how long do you think you can go without taking things seriously? As long as there is emotional investment, people will remain protective of the things they hold dear.

CONDITIONS

Even if there are no preceding conditions, situationship may nevertheless have clauses that control certain circumstances. Usually, these clauses are drafted and understood at the start of the connection, this is until an emotional outburst arises.

Since one or both people in a situational relationship may not be prepared for a long-term commitment, they may try to avoid labels, titles and future planning. You may wonder how these connections begin, it's simple when two people have the same outlook on life and the same objectives, it can come naturally. However, the perfect understanding that comes initially often gets accompanied by stronger feelings, which is where the difficulties arise.

One or both partners in these situations may be considered single (or "taken" in some circumstances), while the dynamics of each situational relationship may be different depending on a number of factors. Alternatively, two persons already in relationships may opt to date with the understanding that they are not committed to each other and will eventually return to their respective spouses. However, as fun and thrilling as it may be or seem, this can be harmful and dangerous for everyone involved in the situation.

Many people are seen establishing their own rules and conditions for the inner workings of their relationships, making it difficult to make broad generalizations about how they all function. We often hear news and accounts of connections that leave us baffled and stunned, so we can admit that these types of relationships have been around for decades.

Naturally, some people would prefer to avoid the heartbreak of dating by diving headfirst into a monogamous partnership, but it appears based on the success rate that modern romantic partnerships rarely pan out the way those involved had hoped.
These kinds of interactions can be hard on a person's life, and it doesn't matter how many guidelines and boundaries are put in place; this is still the case.

SCHEDULES

If you only invest a small amount of time or effort into something, you're more likely to lose interest in it quickly. Individuals who prefer to maintain casual relationships tend to be more adaptable when it comes to scheduling time together. Due to the unpredictable nature of these connections, planning more than a week ahead can be difficult. Additionally, not everyone may be able to take advantage of the current situation.

Genuine romantic attraction often results in lengthier and more meaningful interactions between partners. They go to great lengths to maximize their time together, which they value greatly. Conversely, those involved in short-term relationships may never cross paths again.

The absence of communication between two people who were once close may give the appearance that neither of them is concerned about the other's well-being. It's not always the case; many people who experience these issues already have packed agendas owing to work or other commitments. This could leave little room for putting effort into developing meaningful relationships with others.

As a direct result of this, some people believe that the connections that we have with one another under varying circumstances, such as these, are only superficial.

RATIONALE

Finding oneself in a "situationship" can happen for many different reasons. Perhaps the individual is spending time with someone without any clear intentions or is uncertain about what they wants in a partner. People often use this situation to justify why they are not looking for a committed relationship at the moment. However, if the other person has not introduced them to their close circle after a few weeks or months, it's a clear indication that they are in a situationship. While this discussion typically happens at the start of such an arrangement, it's important to re-evaluate the situation and understand where things stand as time passes.

FUTURE

For some, the beginning of a romantic relationship is a time of immense excitement and anticipation. Some people feel anxious and confused when they consider their current situation. If the other person is significant to you, then being in a predicament where you don't know what to do could increase your stress levels. If you don't see a future with this person and can't see yourself being with them forever, it's better to be upfront and honest about your feelings.

Many people feel the reasons people have extramarital affairs are trivial or even scandalous, but the fact is that many people have them behind closed doors, and some single people have problems sticking to single relationships. Everything that has been said may be boiled down to two fundamental human needs: the need for satisfaction, and the chance to create one's own life. Remember that we're all human and can succumb to egotism and the desire to have one's cake and eat it too.

HAVE YOU BEEN IN A SITUATIONSHIP? (YES) OR (NO)

HOW LONG DID IT LAST? ___________________

PROS: 👍

① ____

② ____

③ ____

CONS: 👎

① ____

② ____

③ ____

WHAT IS YOUR CURRENT SITUATION?

DON'T MAKE EVERYONE YOU DATE, A PARENT!

Quote:

*"Self-respect knows no considerations." - **Mahatma Gandhi***

It's never too late to take stock and make improvements, even if we're having this talk years down the line. There is no downside to learning from mistakes and not making the same ones again. One of the greatest gifts you can give your children and grandchildren is a firm belief in the value of a stable family unit. If you're serious about avoiding being a statistic, now is the moment to empower yourself with as much knowledge as possible.

Don't be shy about benefiting from the experiences and insights of those who came before you. Human connection hasn't altered much over time, as evidenced by reflecting on the lives of people you know or have heard about, even though no two situations are comparable. The best way to face an uncertain future is to know exactly what you want and to avoid giving other people the authority to get in the way of that.

A couple may decide to quit their relationship following the birth of their child, even though all signs pointed to their being happy and secure beforehand. It's true in most situations, but it's especially true once the first child is born, and yet nobody ever talks about it. The birth of a child seems to cause a lot of couples to break up.

How many of your parent-friends do you think are still with the person they had their first child with?

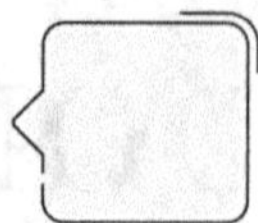

BALANCING ACT

In addition to dealing with "serial baby daddies," or fathers who are unreliable or inconsistent in their involvement in their children's lives, some parents put in significant effort to negotiate complex co-parenting agreements with committed exes. For youngsters whose parents are divorced or separated, seeing other children go home with both parents instead of having to pick can leave them feeling guilty about what they did to deserve this.

For many kids, having two parents at home is more important than having the newest fashions in clothing and shoes. I can't imagine being a single mom and being able to shoulder the responsibility of raising my kids by myself. When a woman decides to raise a family, she normally expects her partner to help out with things like housework and financial obligations. It can be much more difficult if the woman is simultaneously trying to further her degree therefore choosing to have children at a certain point in your life is a major life decision that should never be taken lightly.

The advice I received early in life to "never go into anything depending on others" has served me well, and I try to remember that whenever I am about to take on a major new venture. It's important to go through all the potential outcomes if you ever have to live independently. Today's kids need their parents to spend a lot of time with them and show them the ropes.

PLAYING WITH FIRE

We seem to have to put our hand on the fire these days to know if it's hot or not. We should put as much thought into selecting a life partner as we would into finding a high-paying job. The individual's CV should be informative and entertaining, stressing their greatest attributes and relevant experience in areas such as health, education, employment, and appearance. Many women have similar criteria at first, but these expectations generally dissipate once they believe they have found true love. When you meet a guy, there should be enough incubation time to learn about the person you're getting to know.

Women frequently commit the error of becoming pregnant without first acquiring all of the necessary information. It isn't until the baby is born, and they learn what they should have learned during incubation that they realize their method wasn't particularly well thought out. Almost immediately, both parents develop sudden hate for one another; this is a common occurrence.

It can be harder for adults to focus, manage their money, and establish good habits after the arrival of children. Having children in today's rapidly changing world means that time and money are never on your side. Kids today are asking hard questions that most of us didn't even think of as children, and they are much less accepting of their birth conditions than we were. They have a keen eye for detail and resentment of decisions and circumstances that affect them.

This is why working for one's own growth and development is crucial. Don't settle for a slightly better life as you move forward with your plans. It's important to recognize cycles and break destructive ones to make a fresh start.

REASONING

If a person already has three children from two or more relationships, it may not be in their best interests to have a fourth child. The data shows that if marriage and starting a family aren't possibilities, these patterns virtually never end well. Men often withhold facts from women they believe may force them to reevaluate decisions they've made in their love relationships. Time and evaluation, especially if there is a pattern to the person's behavior, will reveal everything of value about that person. Consider your values, priorities, and beliefs as a parent, and ask yourself some tough questions before making decisions that will affect your child as an adult.

UNFORESEEN CIRCUMSTANCES

While marriage does not ensure contentment, it can make ending a relationship more challenging, especially if children are involved. The emotional and physical well-being of a child may suffer if they are brought up in an unstable or tumultuous environment. Children raised by both parents still have challenges, although they face much less of them.

Children from broken homes may feel divided between two or more sets of values or standards if the rules in each home are different. Having to choose between their parents and being physically removed from one for numerous days, weeks, or months can cause emotional turmoil in a youngster, and this confusion isn't the children's fault. In the event that the parents decide to divorce or live apart from one another, the children should be prepared to spend time with both of their parents in separate environments, whether they like it or not.

Sometimes other members of the family, such as half-siblings or stepparents, are included. While kids usually don't bat an eye at new situations, their parents often do.

It's horrible when parents and kids both have to make decisions they don't like, but understand they need to make for the sake of their kids' safety. The majority of moms are sole caregivers for their children because they find it difficult to leave them with anyone else. However, it is always unjust to keep the children away from the fathers, who have an equal right to them. That's why it's so important to learn as much as possible about the people you're considering having a kid with and their families.

After the baby is born, it's too late to communicate worries and regrets. However, one must make every effort to ensure that every child has the opportunity to grow up in a secure, loving household.

Will the father of your children treat ALL of his children fairly, if he has them from previous relationship(s)? 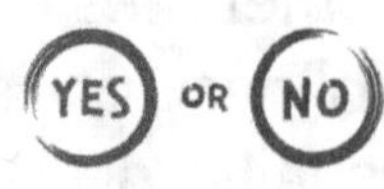

It's generally agreed that both parents should put in a lot of time, energy, and money into their children. However, there are those fathers who are selective in the attention they provide their kids. No mother, regardless of her relationship with the father, should ever condone such cruel treatment of children.

Do you and the man who could father your child share similar values? 
When it comes to raising children, having a spouse who does not share your morals or belief system can have serious consequences and even lead to the end of a relationship. When kids are involved, this becomes even more apparent.

Taking into account all costs, can the family afford to have another child? 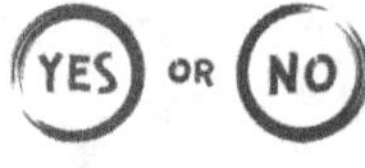
To thrive, children need not only our time and attention but also safe and caring surroundings. As a result of this, arrangements must be made for their care, including giving them a safe place to live, an appropriate education, and enough to eat and wear, without compromising the well-being of other children. Many parents think it's good for their kids to learn to recycle and share resources. However, every kid is unique, and they all require their own space to thrive.

HOW IMPORTANT DO YOU THINK IT IS TO RAISE KIDS IN A TWO-PARENT HOME?

1   **2**   **3**   **4**   **5**

NOT
IMPORTANT

VERY
IMPORTANT

HOW IMPORTANT ARE THE OVERALL POINTS TO YOU?

1   **2**   **3**   **4**   **5**

NOT
IMPORTANT

VERY
IMPORTANT

Where the person you're dating already has kids:

Will you make an effort to get along with the parent(s) of your child's sibling(s)?   YES OR NO

____

____

____

____

How does your partner treat <u>all</u> of his children?

____

____

____

How old are your partner's kids?

____

If any, what are the arrangements for child custody?

____

____

Is the father or mother required to pay child support? (YES) OR (NO)

Are the payments on time? (YES) OR (NO)

Would you ever assist your partner with child support payment(s)? (YES) OR (NO)

What role do you intend to play in the other children's lives? (YES) OR (NO)

WARNING SIGNS

Anger control problems - Stress, interpersonal issues, and material difficulties are only a few common sources of anger. In other cases, an illness like drunkenness, drug abuse, or depression may be the underlying cause. Although anger is a symptom of many types of mental illness, it is not a problem in and of itself. It's important to remember that dealing with someone who suddenly goes from 0 to 100 can cause additional, more serious problems.

Lack of Confidence - Similar to having low self-esteem, this trait is when someone doesn't believe in themselves or what they can do. They often feel unloved, or not good enough. People with low self-esteem always worry about messing up or letting others down, this is a personal problem that you can only do so much to help. Choose wisely.

Narcissism - You probably hear this one often. This character lacks empathy for others, has troubled relationships, a distorted sense of self-importance, and a strong need for unrestrained attention and praise. However, this outward confidence conceals weak self-esteem that is sensitive to even the slightest criticism.

Dominating - Some people like and can handle strong personalities and obedience; however, this is not true for everyone. People's underlying features, such as a strong desire for power and a sense of pride, are most likely the foundation of dominant characteristics. Arrogance, superiority, and conceit are also shown, this spirit can potentially lead to more serious issues, like control and detachment.

Obsessive-Compulsive - A drive for perfection and dominance over others are hallmarks of this personality type. Obsessive thoughts and subsequent behavior help the person feel more in control of their anxieties. It's usually futile to try to persuade someone otherwise because nothing you say or do will sway their opinion.

Isolation - The first sign is the lack of a healthy balance in a relationship or personally. You may notice a person begin staying away from close friends and family or insist that you do. This is usually to ensure the 'victim' becomes extremely dependent on the controlling partner.

Emotional Detachment - This is sometimes caused by past hurt or neglect. It is when a person can't fully connect to their own emotions or the feelings of other people. It might get in the way of a person's physical, mental, emotional, and social growth. This also affects the way they love others and can come off cold and distant.

Low Self-esteem - Some people are masters of concealment. In most cases, this will be the most attractive or best-dressed person in the room, but after spending some time with them, you'll see a striking lack of assurance in their own identity and behavior. They have a constant state of anxiety, awkwardness, or insecurity. People with low self-esteem are typically paralyzed by fears of criticism and failure. Others may find it tiring if you feel the constant need to reassure and motivate them.

Victim - Individuals with a "victim mentality" tend to bring their partners down by constantly complaining about how miserable, worried, and insecure they are. You should take a step back and ask yourself if you are truly feeling this way or if you are simply absorbing the tension of those around you.

Mental, Emotional, or Physical Abuse.
Fighting usually does not begin with physical contact. Abuse often begins slowly, with little things like a few slurs here and there. There may be odd excuses made to block you from seeing loved ones. When people are alone, they are more likely to resort to violence. You begin to feel trapped, and it is not uncommon for verbal abuse to escalate into physical violence, which can be fatal. GET OUT!

Co-dependency - It's a combination of psychological and behavioral symptoms that makes it difficult to maintain positive, fulfilling relationships with others. Those with codependency are more likely to enter or remain in relationships that are unhealthy for them emotionally or physically.

Passive-aggressiveness - This way of thinking is wrong. It's a silly game that hurts relationships and friendships. It is a type of indirect hostility that shows anger and other negative feelings without saying them out loud. Most people respond because they are angry or too shy to talk to the person directly. Many people who use passive aggression may still deny that that was their goal.

Jealousy - Certain behaviors are insignificant, unnoticeable, or discreet. Those who suffer from extreme jealousy are more likely to take violent action. Frequently, they fret over a potential loss or unjust treatment. Some people have a tendency to be possessive of others, especially romantic partners and close friends.

The only option when envy becomes harmful is to seek treatment, yet we all experience it from time to time.

WHICH TRAITS HAVE <u>YOU</u> OBSERVED IN A RELATIONSHIP?

- ☐ Anger control problems
- ☐ Lack of Confidence
- ☐ Narcissism
- ☐ Dominating
- ☐ Obsessive-Compulsive
- ☐ Isolation
- ☐ Emotional Detachment
- ☐ Low Self-esteem
- ☐ Victim
- ☐ Mental, Emotional, or Physical Abuse
- ☐ Co-dependency
- ☐ Passive-aggressiveness
- ☐ Jealousy

WHICH TRAITS DO <u>OTHERS</u> ACCUSE YOU OF HAVING?

- ☐ Anger control problems
- ☐ Lack of Confidence
- ☐ Narcissism
- ☐ Dominating
- ☐ Obsessive-Compulsive
- ☐ Isolation
- ☐ Emotional Detachment
- ☐ Low Self-esteem
- ☐ Victim
- ☐ Mental, Emotional, or Physical Abuse
- ☐ Co-dependency
- ☐ Passive-aggressiveness
- ☐ Jealousy

Minds Notes

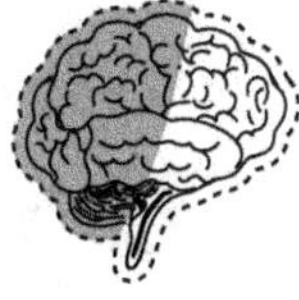

Questions Women Are Asked

Does size matter?

Craziest Experience?

Favorite person?

Nickname?

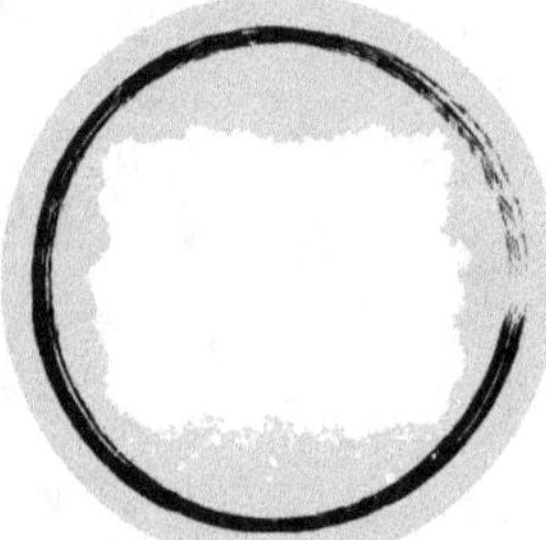

Ever had a One-night stand?

Top or Bottom?

Cuddle or not?

Bodies?

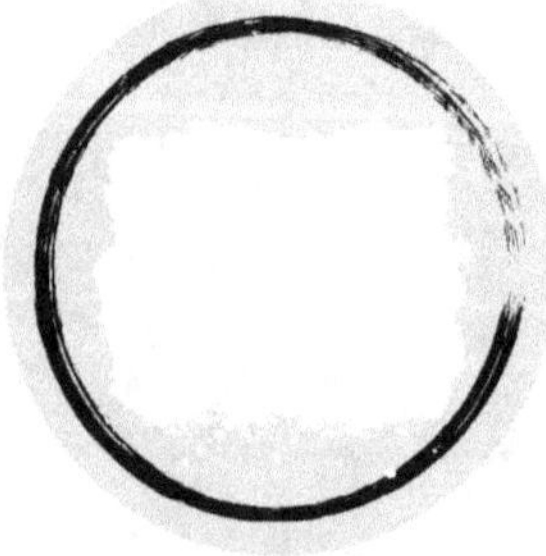

Never ever?

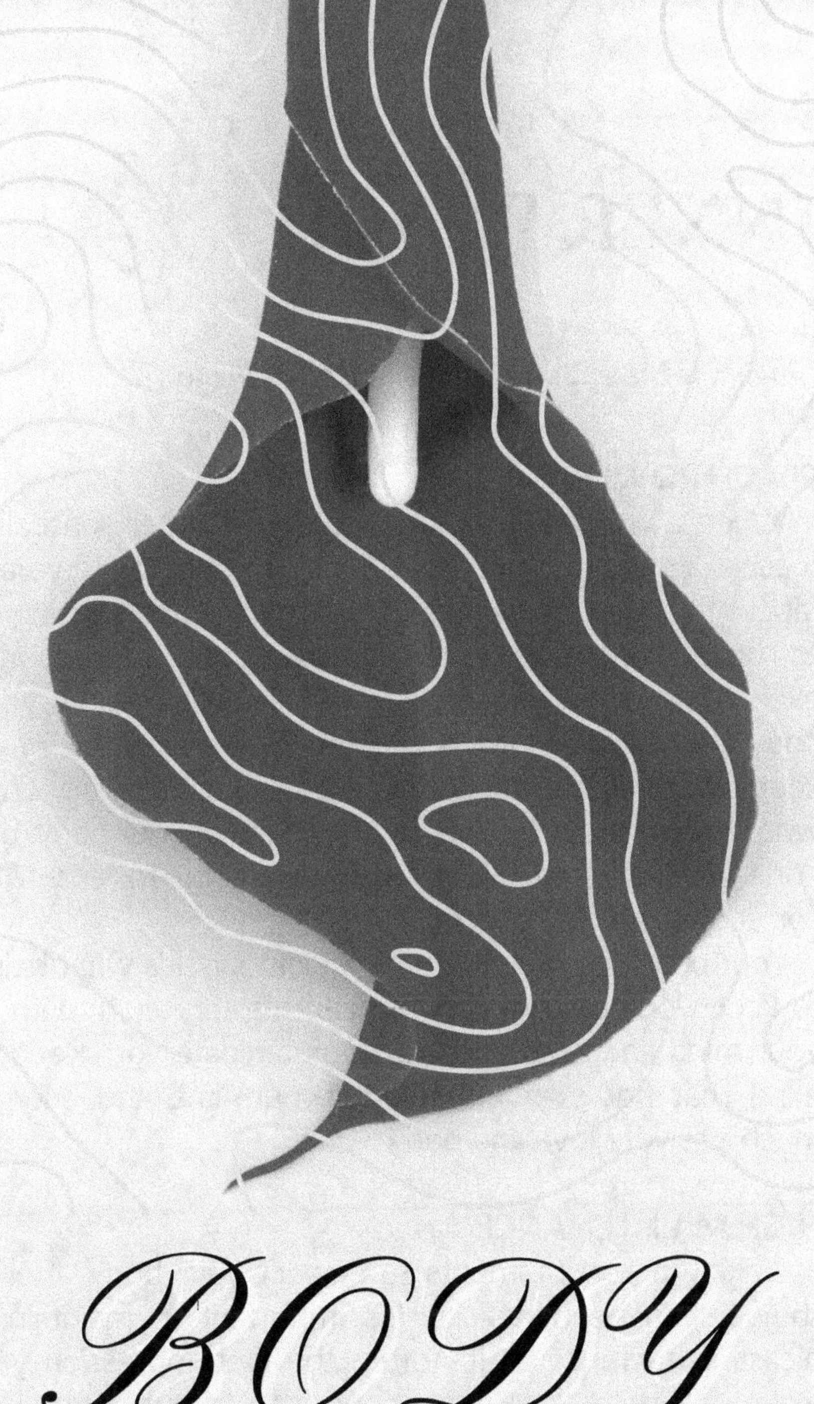

BODY

CHAPTER 2

INNER PEACH

Quote:
"Vagina is the epitome of resilience." - Unknown

PEACH POWER

When a woman embraces her true self, her sensuality reaches its highest potential. From a young age, we are taught to be cautious of strangers touching us, causing us to build barriers around ourselves and neglect the exploration of our bodies. However, learning about your body and its functions is nothing to be ashamed of or keep hidden. You and your gynecologist are the only ones who should have a thorough knowledge of your body, but don't be surprised if they ask questions to ensure a correct diagnosis.

Your peach is as precious as a diamond. It's what helps to keep you going, and if you can master its strength in your mind and soul, nothing will intimidate you. Keep in mind that not everyone merits your time and energy, much less your love and body.

HIGH MAINTENANCE

Taking a few moments to inspect your body after a shower can be beneficial. It's important to maintain a pleasant fragrance as it's often the first impression you make on others. It is not a good idea to put all of your faith in feminine products that will, at best, just provide you with little to no advantages.

It's important to be mindful of how the foods and drinks you consume affect your body. Maintaining a balanced diet that includes both your favorite foods and fresh produce is crucial. Your skin, including that of your intimate areas, will naturally perspire and shed dead cells, so it's important to wash frequently. For cleaning the vaginal canal, water is all that's necessary. While it may seem like promoting personal hygiene products for women has been commercially successful, it can actually have negative social consequences.

ANTI-

It's important to avoid douching to prevent vaginal infections, as it can encourage the growth of yeast and bacteria. Popular items can also upset the vaginal pH balance. If you experience a discharge that looks like cottage cheese, seek medical attention. It's not possible to benefit from the body's own detoxification processes in this area. It's okay to use water for vaginal hygiene after your period is over.

Avoid using vaginal cleansers or deodorants on your underarms to mask any odor coming from your genitals. Your body can develop a tolerance, and sudden withdrawal may lead to the production of unpleasant hormones and odors. If you have vaginal hygiene concerns or notice an unusual odor, it's best to consult a gynecologist.

OH NO!

Due to its delicate skin and soft flesh, peach is an object that should not be mistreated or abused by men or anyone else. You should never engage with or give a platform to men who talk disrespectfully about women and their bodies, especially in public places. It reveals how far along in life they are.

You should treat your body with the same love and attention that you do with your hair and makeup. The way other people treat us is a reflection of how we treat ourselves and how they should treat us.

DAILY

In normal social situations, you should never let your body odor draw attention to itself. Oftentimes, affected individuals are oblivious to the problem since they are unable to detect its odor. If you need to confirm something with absolute certainty, you can always ask a reliable source. A person's level of concern for their own cleanliness may be indicated by the way they dress. Wear cotton underwear night after night and never synthetic. It's important to promptly shower and change out of training or hot-weather attire. Don't use harsh detergents or fabric softeners while doing laundry. A suggestion is to use soap that contains glycerine to clean your laundry, it has no artificial flavors, colors, or preservatives.

All skin types, even the most delicate, may benefit from natural soap because of this. If you must use the restroom during your period, remember to wipe from front to back. When you don't have your period, don't use tampons or pads.

SEX

When engaging in sexual activity, it is recommended to use a water-soluble glycerine lubricant and explore alternatives to latex condoms. If you have a new sexual partner, it's important to get tested for STDs annually. It's wise to abstain from sexual activity until you feel better if you experience any changes in your genital area. Discharges and irritations can be common, so it's best to consult a doctor if you have any concerns. Prior to getting a genital piercing, it's recommended that you speak with a doctor.

To prevent razor burns, ingrown hairs, and other skin irritations, always use a clean razor. It's important to only seek out experienced professionals when getting a piercing or having your genital haircut. It is important to carefully monitor the actions of anyone you have entrusted to handle your body. Make sure that clean and fresh needles and utensils are always used. If you notice anything concerning, do not hesitate to speak up and ask questions. Showing love and respect for your body will encourage others to do the same.

HAVE YOU NOTICED ANY SIGNS THAT INDICATE YOU MAY NEED TO VISIT A GYNAECOLOGIST? YES OR NO

DO YOU GET ANNUAL PAP SMEARS? YES OR NO

DO YOU PERFORM THOROUGH SELF-EXAMINATIONS OF YOUR BODY? YES OR NO

DO YOU FEEL EMPOWERED TO MAKE ALL DECISIONS REGARDING YOUR BODY? YES OR NO

WOULD YOU ALTER YOUR GROOMING HABITS, SUCH AS SHAVING OR WAXING, IF YOUR PARTNER REQUESTED IT? YES OR NO

Notes:

OUTER PEACH

Like a barber's chair that fits all buttocks.

— William Shakespeare

EPIDEMIC

The popularity of extremely large buttocks has skyrocketed over the past decade, and it shows no signs of slowing down. People of all ages have open discussions on the benefits and drawbacks of cosmetic surgery. The topic can be heard from formal conferences to casual get-togethers and online message boards. For others, it's all about finding the right doctor at the right price with the most convenient availability for an appointment. Every day, it demonstrates the ingenuity and willingness of human beings to try new things.

Of course, we've always thought (or known) that some A-listers had beautiful posteriors, and today it seems to be the norm in both the media and our own homes. No one seems to be considering the risks and peculiar outcomes that could arise from these procedures. Tragically, the number of deaths attributable to surgical treatments has recently increased since people are willing to go to extremes and spend huge sums of money to accomplish their aesthetic goals.

This may be helpful information for individuals who are considering receiving one of these treatments in the future, but I am more concerned about the emotional effects of desiring and needing these services.

ARE YOU CONTEMPLATING COSMETIC SURGERY? 

WOULD YOU CONSIDER BRAZILIAN BUTT LIFT (BBL) SURGERY?  

INFLUENCERS

I think even Momma is confused by this turn of events or is just sitting on the sidelines munching popcorn with the rest of us because she never warned us that we might relocate our fat deposits around our bodies. As I continue to live, love, and learn, I realize that life holds more than I ever imagined. It's surprising to see that fat transfer has become a new fashion trend. However, it's important to caution future generations of women about the dangers of relying on one solution and disregarding common sense and the long-term effects decisions today may have on their bodies. What's even more concerning is that cosmetic surgery is increasingly becoming a matter of one's mental and emotional well-being, rather than just physical appearance. To begin, let's examine how this trend has become so widespread.

Numerous women, including notable figures, have experienced detrimental consequences, including death, as a result of butt injections. These procedures originated from the illicit distribution of drugs by untrained individuals in makeshift settings. Social media has heavily influenced beauty ideals, resulting in a desire to conform and present oneself as successful, often at the expense of other considerations.

There have been many stories of people suffering from mental disorders both before and after they had cosmetic surgery. This leads many people to falsely believe they have an issue with their appearance that they feel needs correcting. People who suffer from this disorder may worry about features of their appearance that others, including us, are unable to see or comprehend the need for it. The first sign of this is folks receiving continual procedures, all the way to the point when they are no longer appealing or recognized.

MAINTENANCE

Maintaining cleanliness in one's buttocks area has always been a priority. As children, we dreaded two things the most: having to clean ourselves after using the restroom and having to ask for help because we did it incorrectly. Despite the current state of the world, women are still expected to uphold this practice. There are now more advanced systems available that allow us to use the restroom without touching our bodies.

However, I believe that relying on natural and time-tested processes is the best way to ensure cleanliness. The skin around a woman's buttocks is delicate and susceptible to infections and other forms of contamination, much like the vaginal area. Over time, women have learned the standard practices for preventing illness and disease, such as wiping from front to back.

WOULD YOU BE OPEN TO A LESS EXPENSIVE ALTERNATIVE TO COSMETIC SURGERY? 

WOULD YOU ASK YOUR PARTNER FOR THEIR APPROVAL PRIOR TO GETTING A BBL?

FOR WHAT REASONS MAY YOU CONSIDER COSMETIC SURGERY?

☐ TREND   ☐ CONFIDENCE   ☐ ATTENTION   ☐ CLOTHING

☐ JOB   ☐ SOCIAL MEDIA   ☐ NO REASON   ☐ I WOULD NOT

OTHER: ______________________________

UNDER THE INFLUENCE

Nowadays, having a bigger butt is highly valued by individuals from diverse backgrounds. Many people have varying opinions regarding this trend and are becoming more comfortable expressing their honest thoughts and feelings online. While the BBL trend is particularly noticeable among Black and Hispanic individuals, it is worth noting that people of other ethnicities are also getting this procedure. However, it becomes more noticeable and concerning when the body proportions start to look unnatural and excessive.

People from different cultural backgrounds tend to be more open to trying new things that align with their personal preferences. Interestingly, both men and women are equally interested in this latest trend in cosmetics.

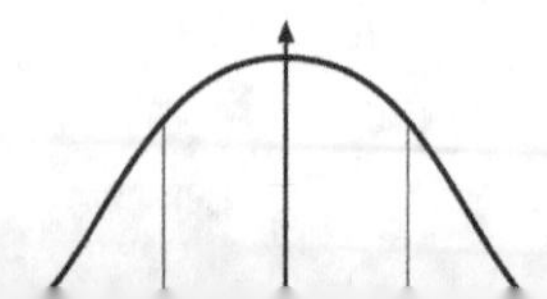

NEW STANDARD

It is widely accepted that having a larger posterior is desirable in two distinct situations: when dressing up and when engaging in sexual activities. This is a commonly held belief that is connected to the media's portrayal of reality and the human tendency to entertain fantasies.

As role models and influencers, continue to struggle with their own imperfections, younger generations are unfortunately exposed to many harmful trends. This has led to the misconception among many young men that a big butt is essential for attracting a good partner. Consequently, young women are often pressured to conform to unrealistic and potentially harmful standards.

SUBSTANDARD

How can married couples, in particular, find common ground among the whirlwind of shifts and development that surrounds us? We'd all prefer it if those who are dear to us were forthright about how they feel and what they want when it comes to issues that come up in their relationships. Also, they would emphasize keeping their word and appreciating their domestic circumstances.

However, the truth is that we live among flawed people who are motivated by their emotions and who adapt to new circumstances in unpredictable ways. Many partnerships fail because their members give in to the temptations of superficiality and materialism. Men are easily swayed by outward appearances, and many women go to great lengths to improve their physical attractiveness in the eyes of potential suitors.

Unfortunately, more and more married women are getting BBL and other cosmetic procedures while paying less attention to their relationships with their husbands and children. To prevent further shame and potential health problems, young women should know that this is not the norm.

It's possible that some people struggle to control their sexual desires and constantly seek new ways to fulfill them, which can create pressure for women to conform to changing sexual expectations. Women face immense pressure to meet these norms and often go to great lengths to do so, while men have generally been able to maintain their individuality despite this pressure. However, men also face their own issues and may sometimes blame women when feeling anxious about something.

Men have the advantage of being able to gain and lose weight at will, voluntarily go bald, and even get cosmetic surgery to replace their hair in recent years. Women sometimes contribute to men holding them to unrealistic physical attractiveness standards.

DO YOU DATE GUYS YOU CONSIDER LESS ATTRACTIVE THAN YOU?

DO YOU BELIEVE THAT SOCIETY PLACES AN EXCESSIVE FOCUS ON PHYSICAL APPEARANCE?

DO YOU THINK THERE IS A DOUBLE STANDARD WHEN IT COMES TO HOW MEN AND WOMEN ARE JUDGED BASED ON THEIR APPEARANCE?

What are your thoughts?

BEST CHOICES

You and your partner may now feel more at ease talking about your bodies and your sexual life and perhaps getting the required tests done. For the first few months, make this a regular component of your schedule. Having an appreciation for one another's tastes helps facilitate decision-making and keep minds focused.

Many women want to be in leadership positions, but they shouldn't unless they've improved their communication skills and created a safe space for everyone involved. Now that you're an adult, I have faith that you'll make healthy decisions for yourself. Study whatever interests you, but focus on topics that pertain to your periphery, such as BBLs, hygiene, anal intercourse, and more.

WAX. LASER. SHAVE. GROW?

"It's not selfish to love yourself, take care of yourself, and to make your happiness a priority. It's necessary."

– Mandy Hale

There has been a shift from DIY hair removal to professional services as the practice gains popularity. Pubic hair is often believed to preserve the delicate skin around the genitalia by reducing friction during sexual activity and other activities. Like the hair on your eyelids and nose, pubic hair acts as a filter, collecting and storing dust, pollen, and bacteria.

SCIENCE

Unfortunately, after shaving the pubic area, there is a higher chance of experiencing vaginal yeast infections, vaginitis, and urethritis. The frequency of waxing or shaving can also increase the risk of skin diseases, such as cellulitis and folliculitis. Additionally, even small injuries that can incur during grooming can result in severe bacterial infections. This highlights the importance of skin care for those who select hair removal techniques; understanding your skin's needs can help you develop a routine that is effective for you. As a result, consulting an expert is recommended.

FUSS

A lady's full body should be respected at all times, including her legs and underarms. It's crucial to keep in mind that hair growth is a natural and healthy occurrence in some cultures, but that doesn't change the fact that it's not regarded as pretty or ladylike in today's society. It's up to you to decide what's best for your body, despite possible shame or condemnation from others depending on your location. Everyone has the right to their own thoughts, behaviors, and perspectives.

WISH

After questioning ten guys, I was able to grasp the significance of body hair in men's perceptions of a potential romantic partner. Many men appreciate a well-groomed private area, but the vast majority prefer the hairless type.

Depending on the texture, some respondents stated they could tolerate a considerable amount of hair, while others said they couldn't.

Here are the responses from the poll:

QUESTION: Which do you prefer in a partner in terms of body hair: someone with hair or someone without hair?

MEN:
3- "No hair! sweat and odor are trapped in hair"
1- "Cleaning hair out of your teeth is not enjoyable"
2- "Bald or very low always looks better to me."
2- "It doesn't matter, once it's well groomed."
1- "Some hair textures and not appealing"
1- "No particular preference"

Some of these statements were funny but not shocking to me, and I think it's important to embrace a person's honesty even if it's difficult to fathom. It can be challenging for many people to date someone who doesn't share their tastes when it comes to the qualities and experiences they're looking for in a mate.

Due to the potential awkwardness of sharing their opinions with women, especially those who are overly sensitive to criticism of their physical appearance, many males keep their thoughts to themselves. But as you get older, you'll learn not to make major life choices without consulting your spouse first and vice versa.

Though you should never feel pressured to make choices about your body, your partner's attitude to your choices may be either supportive or critical. No matter how positive the effects on your health, you must remember that the choice is ultimately yours.

Your decision to keep or remove your beard, body hair, or pubic hair should not be influenced by the opinions of other people. Taking care of one's hygiene and beauty should be the priority. If you know this, you can pick the option that will be best for your health.

When shaving or waxing, more caution and discretion are required. Think of it as an investment and get some expert help to get the greatest outcomes.

Notes:

BEAUTY & SKINCARE

It's incredible what self-care and mindfulness can achieve. The key difference between your skin and someone else's is the investment of equal time and money in their appearance. Having clear skin makes daily life much simpler, once you achieve that goal, you won't need to apply makeup every day, and when you do, it will appear smoother and require less effort.

EXFOLIATE

Keeping your skin clean, fresh, and beautiful is an essential part of any skincare routine, and exfoliation plays a significant role in achieving this. By removing dirt and impurities from your skin, exfoliation unclogs pores, aids in acne prevention, and allows your skin to breathe and restore itself, resulting in a brighter complexion. It's common for people to experience clogging in the nose, chin, and forehead between the eyes. Remember that no skincare product will work effectively if your pores are clogged.

The amount of exfoliation required depends on your skin type. Oily skin may require more frequent exfoliation, such as every other day, to prevent dirt from accumulating in the pores. Dry skin, on the other hand, benefits from exfoliating once or twice a week. If you have mixed skin, an exfoliation regimen that falls somewhere in between the two may work best for you.

Although this is a basic guideline, how frequently you exfoliate your face is mostly determined by the present state of your skin and the environmental factors affecting it. Temperature, air quality, hormones, and age can all play a role in skin diseases. Your skin may feel oilier than usual at times, prompting further exfoliation. Warmer conditions, such as those found in the tropics and the Caribbean, can also have an effect on your skin's appearance.

Sweating causes your pores to clog more readily and frequently. Skin becomes flaky and itchy when there is insufficient humidity in the air. Adapt your skincare routine to the situation. Once or twice a week may suffice on a regular basis, but if you have oily skin or flaky areas, you may need an extra day. Knowing your skin type can assist you in planning your skincare routine but keep an eye on what your skin needs on a daily basis, since it may change.

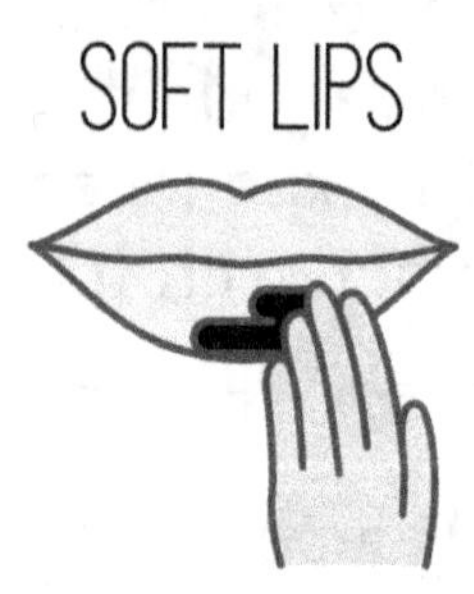

A helpful beauty tip that I often suggest is to exfoliate your lips regularly. This not only benefits the health of your skin but can also improve the quality of your kisses.

To do so, mix whitening toothpaste with brown sugar and gently massage your lips with your fingertips to remove any dead or dry skin.

This can also help brighten your lips, but it's important to only do this when necessary.

 TONING

Toners have been unfairly judged in the past due to the common use of alcohol in traditional treatments. Alcohol is notorious for causing skin dryness, irritations, flare-ups, and premature aging. This is particularly troublesome for people who spend extended periods of time in artificially heated or cooled environments, where they may not consume enough water and indulge in excessive amounts of caffeine and alcohol. These factors can cause the skin to appear dull and lifeless. Nevertheless, a high-quality toner is capable of restoring the skin's natural moisture levels and enhancing its overall appearance.

Your skin's suppleness, smoothness, fine lines and wrinkles, and overall tone can all benefit from proper hydration as part of your daily skincare routine.

The skin's pH can be balanced again with the help of a quality toner. The acidity of your skin can be tested by taking its pH reading, which ranges from 0 to 14, and finding its neutral point, which is 7. Toners restore the skin's natural pH balance, making it healthier and less oily while also making it seem radiant and supple.

The skin is prepped for the next stage, which is the use of a night cream or moisturizer, by first being toned. Applying a cream after you tone will "lock in" the moisture and other benefits of the toner. Use a facial cleanser, toner, and moisturizer. Your complexion will thank you for it.

KEEP IT CUTE!

Maintaining a high standard of personal cleanliness is something everyone should work on, but women in particular will get many benefits from doing so. Whether her hair is natural or enhanced with extensions, a woman who cares about her appearance will keep it clean and smelling nice, wear minimal makeup, and have regular professional manicures and pedicures.

While a man's interest in a woman could be stimulated by the clothes she wore, it's more likely that your hair was the initial focal point of his attention. It's for this reason that it's so important to talk openly and honestly about the profound shifts that inevitably happen in any long-term relationship.

The same goes for men; they should think about how making major changes to their looks will make them feel. When we finally find the person, we want to spend the rest of our lives with, we tend to become more self-absorbed.

When it comes to changes in appearance, women may choose to shave their heads or skip appointments, while men may grow out their beards or experience balding. It's important to recognize that these shifts can have an impact on relationships. Some men prefer women with a natural, low-key look, while others prefer something more attention-grabbing. Women must take good care of their hair if this is important to them. Experimenting with small changes can help you observe your spouse's reaction.

Men may not always express their dislike of a new development and may even make a joke about it. It's worth remembering that men are often attracted to strippers, beautiful celebrities, and attractive servers, regardless of personal opinions. Taking care of yourself can boost your confidence and help you achieve great things. Some men see complacency as a positive because it means less effort on their part. However, it's important to recognize your influence and use it to your advantage before others do.

Notes:

WORKOUT!

Quote:
"The hard part isn't getting your body in shape. The hard part is getting your mind in shape."

Let's resolve to be more mindful of our health this year. When you finish a workout, do you take a moment to appreciate how great you feel? being, physical fitness is a sign of dedication and sexual appeal. It's fascinating to see how much information you can glean about a person without hearing a single word from them.

Workout demonstrates:
- COMMITMENT
- DEDICATION
- STRENGTH
- SELF LOVE
- SELF CARE
- PATIENCE
- APPEAL

Engaging in physical exercise can have a positive impact on our self-esteem and energy levels through the release of endorphins in the body. It is important to establish a workout routine that is realistic for your lifestyle and schedule. If you require additional motivation, consider hiring a personal trainer or enrolling in a group fitness program. Everyone deserves to experience the benefits of feeling good and energized.

HOME

For this year, your goal is to improve your heart health and lose weight. Investing in some exercise equipment can be a good way to help you achieve your goals. There are several exercises that you can do from home, such as arm curls, lunges, push-ups, and squats, which are effective in achieving your goals.

Resistance training has several physical benefits, including increased strength and endurance. It also has psychological and emotional benefits and can enhance your libido. These benefits are a direct result of the increased testosterone levels that result from engaging in such exercise.

SEX & WORKOUTS

Sex is more pleasurable and satisfying when you look and feel well. You'll relax into your own skin and find that some sex positions come naturally to you. You should make the bedroom sessions exciting for both of you by trying out different and new positions (men enjoy them!). Bear in mind that there are plenty of other motivated and capable females out there who would love to take your place. It is, however, your responsibility to achieve results.

It's crucial for women to be realistic and take some responsibility if a man is pursuing them for the same physical traits that attracted them in the first place. As a woman, you should never downgrade yourself to the level of someone a man would settle for. GET TO WORK!

Notes:

Notes:

AVOID UNPROTECTED SEX... UNLESS!

Quote:
"No glove, no love" - Unknown

ROULETTE

Unquestionably! Numerous individuals engage in sexual activity without using contraception due to personal reasons. Sometimes, it seems, for no good reason at all. Some people would rather play Russian roulette with their health, while others are convinced that condoms impair the experience for both partners.

Many men use unprotected sex as a method to show their partners how much they care about them and to solidify their place in the relationship. Some guys become demanding or threaten to end relationships if women don't give in to their demands. But as you may have seen, when it comes to proposing or outlining plans for the future of their relationships, these same guys rarely exert the same type of pressure. One must examine their motives and consider whether or not they are seeking a serious, committed relationship.

Sadly, after they've coerced a woman into unprotected sexual activity, they repeat the act with several other women, and the only way the first lady finds out is if she or one of the other women involved in the act becomes pregnant. Many guys stubbornly refuse to acknowledge this flaw in the masculine psyche. To keep their sexual partner pleased, many women will go to great lengths, but who is watching out for them?

Relationships characterized by risky behavior can lead to several undesirable outcomes, including depression, sexually transmitted diseases, and unintended pregnancies.

GAMBLE

The majority of sexual interactions do not need much planning or preparation since almost everyone has at least one trustworthy sexual partner and each of those partners also has at least one reliable sexual partner.

Good-hearted people sometimes overestimate the honesty and integrity of others around them and address severe matters with a lack of seriousness.

Many tragic events, especially those that take place in social situations, include the use of alcohol or drugs. When deciding to have sexual relations with another person, people need to examine not just their intentions, but also their expectations. Regardless of your romantic state, you still need to pay close attention to your health and the things you allow to be done to your body. It's not always malice that leads to consequences; often, careless optimism and rash choices are to blame.

Don't believe anyone who tells you that you're doomed to contracting a sexually transmitted disease (STD) because of your age or your location. Contrary to promiscuity, though, being in a stable, committed relationship makes you less susceptible to picking up on unwanted signals.

Celibates are the only individuals who never have to worry about sexually transmitted illnesses, and that peace of mind is priceless regardless of what the rest of the world is doing.

It must be awful for young people just starting out since it seems like every day brings a new event that threatens their life. During this time, they are also dealing with the hormonal and social stresses that come with puberty. This is why kids need a safe space where they may feel comfortable speaking up and sharing their ideas without fear of judgment or ridicule.

FIVE STARS

No one should accept a person into their lives, let alone their bedroom, who shows no regard for their own or your health. You should not put your trust in someone who claims to be in a monogamous relationship or married but who is also engaging in potentially unsafe behavior.

Some people think the situation isn't as bad as it seems or that problems can be easily fixed. This casual approach is alarming, as it exemplifies the fact that not all wounds can be completely healed and not all diseases can be cured. Therefore, carefully consider it, taking into account all that is pertinent to your particular position. Create your own set of standards and norms and make it a point to follow them religiously. Never give anyone the power to decide your future.

When we were younger, Momma did her best to avoid these conversations, and we were strictly forbidden from bringing up subjects that were deemed "adult conversations." However, as the world and this generation evolve, things are different now.

The evolution of technology thrusts sexuality into everyone's consciousness; not even cartoons are immune. It is our responsibility as current and future parents, guardians, and moms to anticipate the needs of today's youth so that we can better guide them in the years to come. They need you to reassure them that they are not alone, that it is okay to be yourself, and that it is okay to speak the truth because their peers, social media, and television are all putting in additional effort.

Notes:

3 IS A CROWD!

Quote:

A mind that is stretched by a new experience can never go back to its old dimensions." - Oliver Wendell Holmes, Jr.

The idea that three is too many is not new, and the fact that it is an odd number serves as a useful reminder that even numbers are sufficient for most purposes. Even whether we consider counting objects, playing games, or thinking about our friendships. When dealing with odd numbers, there is always one more than one less. This remains true despite the passage of time.

In relationships both partners may hold strongly individualistic views about the dynamics of their union and their lifestyles. Some people, especially women, feel they have to sacrifice everything for their partners' gratification, and this can lead to risky sexual behaviors that might disrupt or even end a relationship. Yet each individual has the autonomy to choose their own set of beliefs, boundaries, and preferences, so what benefits one person may not benefit another. Both research and common knowledge imply that sexual taboos like threesomes might be harmful to a couple's intimacy and happiness. Always keep in mind that individuals can turn bitter, insecure, and resentful when things don't go their way (or even when they do).

FIGHTING TEMPTATIONS

If a couple doesn't spend a lot of time together, isn't particularly close, or isn't in a serious partnership, they may find the thought of bringing in another person interesting.

The intensity of emotions like a new love or the need for an immediate thrill can cause people to make quick decisions that have lasting consequences.

Bringing new people into a happy and tranquil relationship isn't always as easy as it looks on TV. What happens when feelings emerge as a direct result of sexual encounters, and the only people who can do something about it are the persons directly involved? Taking a step back and looking at the big picture is necessary if you want to keep your relationship on the right track.

PRICE

A quick poll of ten guys revealed that the vast majority of them were opposed to incorporating a third person in their sexual relationship. A couple of them, though, acknowledged playing in a threesome under more informal and experimental situations. Others were apprehensive to do it with a woman they adored, intended to marry, or who was already their wife, whilst others were ecstatic as long as their partner approved.

Those who rejected it indicated a lack of desire as well as anxiety that their spouse would seek pleasure elsewhere and without their knowledge in the future. Given the sensitivity of the matter and the fact that men have different expectations of women's behavior than they do of men's, their replies were unsurprising. If they are not present or consent, the idea of their girlfriend or wife having another man may be humiliating and distressing to them.

This twisted hypothesis stems from the fact that men feel they are less likely than women to become emotionally attached as a result of sexual experiences; they believe they have superior emotional control.

I contend that your partner has emotionally checked out of the relationship if he's willing to sleep with someone else, or he's interested in someone other than his current spouse, or he honestly believes that the bedroom requires something new and exciting to happen to keep things interesting. *How will you know the genuine reason? Ask!*

Some couples might struggle with having a third person in the relationship, while others might thrive with one. Trying something new is not unheard of for a couple on the verge of breaking up. However, remember that altering a preexisting system always results in unintended outcomes. The question is, of course, what the repercussions will be.

Are you open to trying new fantasies?　　YES OR NO

<u>ONE</u> thing that is allowed and not allowed during the encounter:

____

____

____

What do you hope to gain by participating in this activity?

____

____

____

Is your partner interested in sexual fantasies? Ask!　　 YES OR NO

Notes

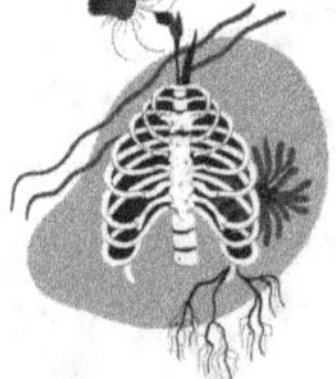

SOUL

CHAPTER 3

30 DAY

Self-Care Challenge

DAY 1	DAY 2	DAY 3	DAY 4	DAY 5
Start a gratitude journal	Meditate	Social media free day	Call someone you love	Take a 20 minute walk outdoors
DAY 6	**DAY 7**	**DAY 8**	**DAY 9**	**DAY 10**
Listen to a talkshow or podcast	Try a new recipe	Stretch for 10 minutes	Listen to your favorite song	Practice deep breathing (5 mins.)
DAY 11	**DAY 12**	**DAY 13**	**DAY 14**	**DAY 15**
Home Workout	Start your manuscript	Write a list of short-term goals	De-clutter a room or desk	Go to bed 1 hour earlier
DAY 16	**DAY 17**	**DAY 18**	**DAY 19**	**DAY 20**
Plan a game night	Wake up 15 minutes earlier	Make your favorite meal	Buy yourself something nice	Create a bucket list
DAY 21	**DAY 22**	**DAY 23**	**DAY 24**	**DAY 25**
Watch a movie or series	Note your ideas	Recommend this book to someone	Have a home spa day	Read inspirational quotes
DAY 26	**DAY 27**	**DAY 28**	**DAY 29**	**DAY 30**
Donate something	Spend some time outside	Do a Face mask	Read a new book	Take a power nap

FIND A HIGHER POWER THAN YOURSELF

Quote:

"To thine own self be true" - William Shakespeare

Humanity has been researching the universe for centuries in a effort to better understand our ultimate creator. However, we won't go that far; instead, we'll look within ourselves, where the journey should have begun in the first place.

What exactly is a higher power?

Higher power can be anything you choose to believe in, so the answer depends on your personal beliefs. Everything, including the natural laws, mathematical concepts, the workings of the human mind, religious doctrines, existentialism, Buddhist philosophical inquiry, and scientific investigation. Despite this, the majority of us had our early education and religious upbringing shaped by the beliefs and practices of our parents when we were younger. Since they were taught about it from the time, they were young, the vast majority of people continue to engage in the same religious or spiritual practices that they were taught when they were children. Those who adhere to a specific religion or philosophy may regard their deity as being superior to those of other faiths and philosophies.

It has been understood in two very distinct ways: the first is as an allusion to the supreme entity that was responsible for creating the world, and the second is as a metaphor for emptiness. A person can learn to identify a higher spiritual entity in one's life even if they do not subscribe to the concept that God is the highest spiritual being. This is the case with the great majority of individuals around the world.

The concept of a higher power should be personal and distinctive to every person. Even if everyone has their own set of beliefs, you should never try to impose anything on someone else; rather, you should have conversations with people who are also on a spiritual journey to gain fresh perspectives and viewpoints. Practice wisdom and meditation to cultivate clarity in your thinking. Those who are patient and attentive to their surroundings have a better chance of discovering a greater power.

You are the one accountable for determining your path and bringing peace along with it, others will see the higher power in you through your life's work.

WHAT DO YOU BELIEVE?

WHAT ARE YOUR THOUGHTS ON LIFE AFTER DEATH?

SOUL TIES

Flee also youthful lusts: but follow righteousness, faith, charity, peace, with them that call on the Lord out of a pure heart.

-2 Timothy 2:22

It's not a new idea to think that our souls are connected to those of other people. Usually, it means a very close emotional bond between individuals which has been established through personal encounters. Although physical contact can strengthen preexisting ties, many are unaware that soul bonds can be forged in other ways as well.

We have been enabled to cope with these connections for decades without having a clear idea of what they are or why certain circumstances keep occurring.The unwillingness of one partner to move on from previous relationships is a common cause of conflict in intimate and sexual partnerships. People's inability to make good decisions and restrain their emotions was a major contributor to domestic strife for a long time.

When two people share a sexual soul connection, it can lead to destructive emotions and behaviors, such as going to great lengths to get what they think they want. This is because unresolved emotional issues might cause one person to want to exert control over another or foster a dependency mentality. If someone can control or manipulate you without your knowledge, they have a powerful soul tie. Additionally, it may put your future relationships at risk. For example, if you were in a situation where you were ready to move on from a relationship but you were stopped from doing so, this may put your future relationships at risk.

RECOGNIZING

A soul connection exists when there is an unusual degree of intensity between one or both people, regardless of the outcome of the relationship. Relationships often begin because two people have a lot in common; this is especially true for individuals whose shared experiences have been primarily unpleasant and have caused them to radiate dark energy that draws others with similar perspectives. Some of the most poisonous relationships in history can be traced back to this phenomenon, which is called trauma bonding.

From the inside, it might not feel like you have an unusual connection to someone, however many who are around you or know you well will spot it before you do. Usually, these bonds were forged over time because of the substantial impact this person has had on your life, it could be easiest during your vulnerable times. The connection may not have terminated along with the relationship.

HOW TO TELL IF YOUR SOUL IS TIED

The effects of a breakup might last for years, but there are ways to determine if your spirit is truly bound to the person you once loved. Some possible triggers include hearing the person's voice or having them come into your thoughts regularly, especially during the day, in your nightmares, or upon waking.

It's possible that the warning signals of a soul tie could develop serious enough to impact your current or future romantic partnerships. Even to the point where you can find yourself fantasizing about your ex during sexual encounters or passionate moments with your current spouse.

This suggests that severing a soul tie is essential before continuing with your life, and that acceptance is the first step on this path. This problem may also show up in the relationships of people you know, such as family or friends, or even in the friendships your children form. Keep in mind that soul connections don't have to be sexual; sometimes they can form out of pure friendship, especially if the two people involved spend a great deal of time together.

Note: The importance of balance in your daily life.

SEVERING A SOUL TIE

This behavior may be categorized as an addiction, as it has similar traits and actions but further investigation into its causes and effects may be required. While it could be helpful to talk to others about your challenges, it would be more purposeful to focus on changing your behavior. Once you've established the existence of the connection, it's time to weigh the pros and cons it's brought into your life.

Accepting the truth of the situation is the first step in fixing it. Examine the ingrained routines that you will need to start disrupting. Even if it requires separation, suspension, or simple re-routing of contact. Realize that the soul tie was not formed overnight so it may require more time and effort to severe. Seek out professional counseling if you feel you need additional support.

FORGIVENESS

This is often the most difficult step to take, but forgiveness is necessary in the healing process. Under these conditions, it is reasonable for you to believe that the other party to the bond ought to be begging for your forgiveness. Perhaps the other person has done nothing to merit genuine forgiveness.

Forgiveness, in any instance, is discovering and settling any unresolved mental "debts" that may be maintaining a subconscious connection. To do so, you yourself may need to forgive yourself for decisions you've made in the past, which can be a very challenging task.

RELEASE

Finally, get rid of any material that could be used to identify you with another person. Things you like, pictures you save "just in case," and so on are all examples of this category. These symbolize the shackle, and they must be broken. Visualization exercises, in which you imagine the bond between you and the other person and then see that bond cut through the power of your own will and will, are a powerful tool for breaking any and all ties for good. Once you've done away with all of the marks, mental commitments, and spiritual links, you should be on your way to freeing yourself from the effects of a soul bind.

Do you believe in soul ties? 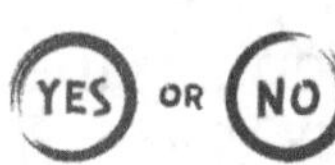

Are you aware of anyone who may feel they are tied to you? 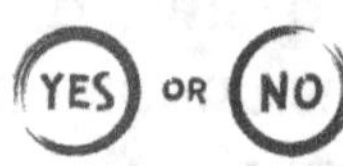

Use five words to describe how you felt after your last breakup.

298

Are you emotionally, spiritually, or sexually linked to anyone?

TIES TO THE SPIRIT:

Write down the names (or initials) of the people—friends, relatives, associates or lovers—with whom you share a deep connection.

BOND - *Strong feelings of affection, trust, and concern*

_______________________   _______________________

_______________________   _______________________

PROTECTIVE - *Concern for safety or need to help*

_______________________   _______________________

_______________________   _______________________

BIND - *Connected by a promise or secret*

_______________________   _______________________

_______________________   _______________________

DEATH - *Bound to the deceased person*

_______________________   _______________________

_______________________   _______________________

SEXUAL - *Difficulties going forward, fixation, yearning, despair*

_______________________   _______________________

_______________________   _______________________

PLAN:

Your word for the month will be the first word you see:

```
JGLOFDJIEMPAPOEOVMSCMWOOPRYTLSMLFJOPRAISEOIL
LOKOGJKLMSMIEOPJMISMMGKEJSKNMLESSONSJAPQDSBI
PEICREATIONJMXLAMFAJFLSMCGJIWLOVEPJIFLAMVLISIV
WILFEGMLEMFMEPABNZLSHUMUOKUITEWJIKOKNVICESBN
UMSNGKDSLJGKDLSJGKLSGRATITUDEJGKLSJAKLGZVMOP
NWORKWUODLOPWSJGOSKIEMNBSKGMNBAXBOMSIIDGEV
TIMELNGSANVOCONNECTIONKMGEWJNNZCMANHHELPNGA
NOIRPWIOTYIEJCZXNMXZVJSACKSMZNVLGKELJWJKJDEIIC
INSNJOORWADEXCRPWVGCRBYTHMONEYKIUMLIMLYCURIA
UJURNWCGEYVOPOWERPUIYXORWKLJOSKLGJNDSLIJISTIT
CETALIGNMENTJEMISLJJFLSHAHMLFJELWPORIMSOMJLBFI
YIMCESKOGJKLMSMIEOPJMLSMVMGKEJSKNMJAPOPEFHJNO
SOMXLAMFAHEALTHJFLSMCGJIWPJFLAMVLWIFEGMGMIHIIN
HNNMFMEPAVBNZLSNMJOKUISELFCAREVMSNGKDSLGRTIF
OJGADLSJGKLSJGKLSJAKLGZUNMCNSJWUODLOPWSJDLI
PGDRKIEMNBSKGMNBAXBDMSGMELNGSANVDSMGEWLCUI
JNNRCMANHHFLSTRENGTHWOIRPWIOIYIEJCZIMANIFEST
XZVISAGKSMZNVLGKELJWJKCNSNFAMILYUDORSLEEPOAJ
WXARSWVGCRYLTNKUMLIMLYBJVRNWCGEYVOXDRWSNMI
QLGDSKLWPURPOSEJKDSLJEMJGLDMGKOMSDOEOVMJJKI
STEWOOMIRACLESPRYTSMIFJOMCESKOGJKLMSMIGRJYTI
IELPJMLSMUMGKEJSKNMJAPOBREAKTHROUGHPEIJMYOUI
KLAMFAJFLSGMDTPRAYERSDKABNPOIUMAFNHAHUHYITFI
JUMJJOHJSWURUMAMBOGEHJAKOWHCSANKNLALADIRUNI
```

YOUR WORD OF THE MONTH:

YOUR WORD OF THE MONTH:

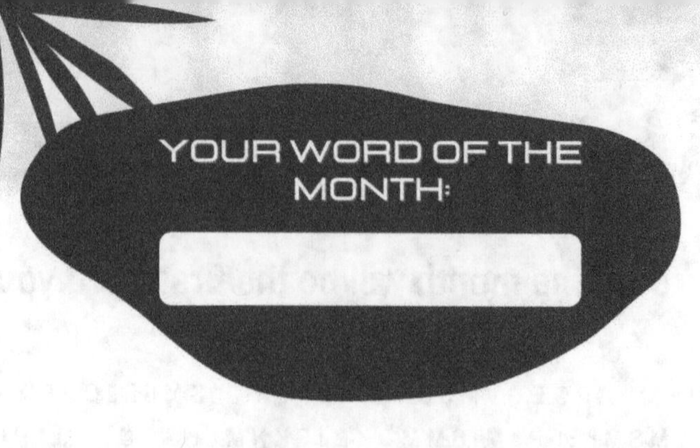

How does the word apply to your present circumstances?

GENERATIONAL!

Quote:

" You only live once, but if you do it right, once is enough."
— Mae West.

At various stages in one's life, the burden of one's ancestors can be both an advantage and an impediment. The idea of ancestral sin, also known as generational sin or ancestral blame, holds that descendants bear responsibility for the sins of their forebears. While we have no say over our biological families, we do get to choose our adoptive ones, because it's one thing to know someone and quite another to truly care for them. Commitment, genuine affection, and looking out for one another's best interests are what turn a group of people into a family.

WHAT THE HEX?

Despite your notion that it is difficult to discern what is situational and what is related to your family history if you see patterns that have been passed down from generation to generation, it is permissible to claim it is a curse. The word "curse" has a negative connotation, but there are many things that happen to people that cannot be explained or solved.

The Bible contains numerous examples of a curse being placed on the next generation because of the sins of the current one. While some may always refuse to believe it, those who have seen or experienced it for themselves can speak to its reality. Identifying a curse's symptoms is the first step toward overcoming its hold.

FAMILY TIES

It is possible to transmit not only physical traits but also mental and spiritual qualities from one generation to the next. The outcomes are completely open to interpretation! Finding the origin of a curse can be helpful in preventing it from happening again. As a result of their disobedience, God cursed a few people in the Bible, thus it's safe to assume that cursing is an old custom. Although some family members may be aware of the existence of such curses, most of them likely are not, leading them to believe that the ill fortune of their ancestors will continue for years to come.

Have you ever considered that maybe people's terrible luck isn't so much the result of fate as it is of their own foolish actions?

These are some ways in which curses may manifest:
Unhealthy relationships: Divorces, strife, death, jealousy, envy, incest, rage, drugs and alcohol addiction.
Health issues: Cancers, mental illness, barrenness and impotency.
Witchcraft: Rejection, instability, physical abuses, poverty, stagnation, secrets, financial attacks, suicide and sexual promiscuity.

10 FAMILY CURSES

SPOKEN WORDS

We all say things to one another every day, whether we mean to or not, and most of the time we don't give any thought to the potentially life-altering impact of our words.

People today say the cruelest things to one another, suggesting that they have lost their capacity for empathy.

- *"Damn you"*
- *"It doesn't matter what you try, you just can't succeed"*
- *"You cannot be saved."*
- *"You fool"*
- *"Dummy"*
- *"You are so stupid."*
- *You're ugly.*
- *"You're hopeless"*
- *"You'll never learn"*
- *"Go to hell"*

No matter how others treat you, even irate parents can be guilty of this. Always remember:

God is the source of your power, and the Bible has passages to remind you that He made you in His image, making you full and perfect just as you are. By His favor, you are not a fool but rather wise, for he will teach you everything you need to know to live in paradise for all of eternity.

WEALTH

If forced to choose just one curse, most individuals would go for some form of wealth. Having a lot of money can be both an enabling and a gift, depending on how you utilize it. However, God commands you to provide as much assistance as you can to the next generation. If misfortune is linked to financial matters, then family feuds may occur over property and inheritance. Many parents fail to correctly label the gifts they give to their children, causing unnecessary sorrow and anxiety that can linger for generations.

While no one has any right to another person's possessions, parents do have a responsibility to provide generational wealth to their children and their children's, children giving them the best opportunity to flourish and carry on the family's good fortune appropriately and beneficially.

Is your family wealthy from generation to generation?   

CAST

To be able to break generational curses, you must first admit that there is a problem in your family. Ignoring the problem will not make it go away; in fact, doing so will make the situation worse in the long run. This is something to keep in mind, particularly if you have young children or grandchildren.

One of the trickiest parts of the challenge is figuring out what the curse is and then declaring it aloud. You will need help, whether from a spiritual leader or a therapist, to break family curses that have been passed down through the years.

They will advise you on how to approach the situation, but before you address others, you should get treatment for yourself. Everyone will not be open to it, but you will have done your part. Remember, it is not your fault that these patterns exist, but it is within your power to work towards changing them for the better.

Do you believe in generational curses? YES OR NO

Are there any obvious patterns affecting your family? YES OR NO

Can you openly address your issues with your family members? YES OR NO

What are the barriers to your family's generational wealth?

Notes:

carpe diem!

This coming new year, I will:

____

____

____

____

____

____

____

____

____

____

____

DO MENTAL HEALTH CHECKS OFTEN!

Quote:

"You gotta train your mind to be stronger than your emotions or else you'll lose yourself every time."

OPEN UP

So when was your most recent therapy session?

You do know that this is perfectly healthy and normal, right?

YES OR **NO**

Despite the social stigma that surrounds seeking professional psychological or therapeutic help, everyone occasionally needs a place to unload their emotions. It's normal to vent to loved ones about the ups and downs of life, but a trained expert is the best person to talk to because they'll know the correct questions to ask and will have sound advice to provide.

This is perfectly normal and appropriate despite the social stigma attached to seeking help from a psychologist or therapist, everyone needs somewhere they can go to unload their emotions every once in a while. It's normal to vent to loved ones about the ups and downs of life, but a trained expert can ask the proper questions and offer sound guidance.

MAN IN THE MIRROR

Many of us are hard on ourselves and always find something wrong, which makes us doubt ourselves. You need to be friends with both your inner critic and your external cheerleader. Find a balance between the two energies by being careful, kind, respectful, honest, and fair. Just like you would want others to treat you.

OPEN UP

Some therapists say that while teamwork could be good, everyone must work on themselves independently in order to become whole mentally and emotionally. The search for meaning and satisfaction is crucial for human development as well as physical and mental health. Before chasing happiness, we must recognize that it, like all other emotions, is changeable.

When looking for professional help, it's important to be picky about whom you hire. There are professionals out there who are really good at what they do and should have a track record. Don't give anyone the chance to use your weakness against you. Make an appointment as soon as you can, because the cost is well worth it.

ARE YOU HAVING TROUBLE LOVING AND ACCEPTING YOURSELF?   YES OR NO

WHAT ABOUT YOU DON'T YOU LIKE?

WHAT STEPS WILL YOU TAKE TO ADDRESS YOUR PERSONAL CONCERNS?

 # SELF CHECK IN: ___________ 

HOW ARE YOU ACTUALLY FEELING TODAY?

PHYSICALLY AND MENTALLY:

____

____

____

WHAT IS TAKING UP MOST OF YOUR MENTAL SPACE RIGHT NOW?

____

____

____

WHAT WAS YOUR MOST RECENT COMPLETE MEAL?

____

HAVE YOU DRANK ENOUGH WATER TODAY?   YES OR NO

DO YOU SLEEP WELL?   YES OR NO

HOW MANY HOURS ON AVERAGE?

WHAT HAVE YOU BEEN DOING TO STAY FIT?

WHAT DID YOU DO TODAY TO MAKE YOU HAPPY?

WHAT HAVE YOU BEEN DOING TO STAY FIT?

WHAT DID YOU DO TO MAKE YOURSELF HAPPY TODAY?

IN THE COMING MONTHS, WHAT DO YOU MOST ANTICIPATE?

WHAT ARE YOU GRATEFUL FOR RIGHT NOW?

A CHOICE ALWAYS EXISTS!

"Don't make a permanent decision based on temporary emotions." -Unknown

Keeping calm and letting things go when they become overwhelming is a skill that will serve you well in many situations. Too many people have shown their emotional instability in their interactions with others and the problems they create for themselves. There is never a good reason to cause bodily or emotional anguish to oneself, other people, or animals, no matter how legitimate you feel the cause may be.

If you find yourself in a predicament or received unexpected news, don't rush into things; instead, work on strengthening your mind, heart, and ability to deal with stress. Effective strategies for developing fresh methods of handling problems include honest self-evaluation and reaching out for support when necessary.

IMPULSE

Particularly if you react emotionally or impulsively, based on deeply held values, this could set off a domino effect of negative feelings and terrible assessments about yourself and your life. This is especially the case if your reaction is emotional or spontaneous and based on deeply held values and convictions.

We may sometimes share a desire to see wrongdoers face the consequences of their acts, regardless of how closely or widely they correspond with our ideals. It's tough to stay positive when we're constantly being bombarded by negativity. Many people are currently dealing with the consequences of decisions they made in the past without carefully considering all of their options because of emotional impulses and the human predisposition to respond impulsively.

I had learned from prior experiences that the environment I created and the people I associated with led to an unpleasant sensation in the areas that I frequented. I came to the conclusion that the most important adjustment I needed to make in my life was to sever those relationships and establish a new atmosphere that radiated light. It was the finest decision I'd made in the past since it allowed me to devote more of my time and effort to things that were essential.

EVALUATION

When two emotions seem so in conflict with one another, it may help the mind focus on the one that is closer to the truth or what makes logical sense. If you have strong feelings, relationships, viewpoints, or ideas, it may be difficult to accept this harsh reality. However, it's important to consider other people's perspectives as well whenever possible; doing so will broaden your understanding of the problem.

The way you act will change dramatically once you learn to translate your gut feelings into deliberate, methodical behavior. This is some advice I frequently give and take to heart myself. You'll have a more positive view and find joy in everyday activities.

BEST CHOICES:

- Compare yourself to no one.
- Build a team of advisors.
- Guard your good name.
- Trust your instincts.
- Get rid of your bad habits.
- Ask for help.

WHAT EMOTIONAL REACTIONS ARE YOU WORKING ON?

BALANCE IS...

Quote:

*Life is like riding a bicycle. To keep your balance, you must keep moving." - Albert Einstein

Finding a happy medium between your job and free time is essential to your health and happiness in all aspects of your life, whether interpersonal, professional, dietary, or spiritual. An overflowing cup is a powerful symbol of the havoc that can be caused by too much of anything. In the same vein, if you don't try to accomplish anything, life might become routine and uninteresting. Creating reasons to be alive and useful makes everyday living worth it. However, everyone has a distinct concept of what makes for a well-rounded life, and if you want to be happy and healthy, it's important to figure out what that is for you.

It's easy to lose sight of what matters when we're so preoccupied with trying to make it big financially and live the life of our dreams. Before we realize it we would of either expend all of our time and energy, be too exhausted to do anything when we return home, or we will have lost all of our opportunities.

We all have perfect examples of when we missed special events, recitals, or celebrations because work came first. Unfortunately, we don't feel guilty about ignoring others until they're no longer here to make the few hours we devote to them each week seem inconsequential. When it happens, it may be too late to do anything about it.

Find Your Balance: Building Better Connections in a Chaotic World

In a world where we juggle countless roles and responsibilities, it's no surprise that we prioritize certain people over others. But here's the thing: relationships are like houseplants—they need attention, care, and sometimes a little TLC to come back to life. Without regular effort, even our most meaningful connections can wither away.

Investing time and energy into fostering genuine relationships isn't just a nice-to-have—it's essential if we want to thrive. Yet, our culture often encourages us to live in extremes—whether it's chasing the perfect aesthetic, curating our social circles, or obsessing over food trends. Without boundaries, things can spiral out of control. Add the internet to the mix, where misinformation spreads unchecked and accountability is scarce, and it's easy to see why so many of today's issues feel overwhelming. If we don't shift course, the chaos could deepen, leaving future generations to pick up the pieces.

Finding balance is a skill we must pass on. It's about teaching ourselves and others that peace of mind isn't something that just happens—it takes work, intention, and a commitment to finding equilibrium.

Stress is a major culprit behind so many of today's health struggles. When life feels like a mess, the ripple effects can impact our bodies, emotions, and mental clarity. But when you achieve balance, everything snaps into focus. You can make intentional choices about what truly deserves your energy and what you're better off letting go.

For women, especially, the pressure to do it all can be overwhelming. Many of us take on more than we can handle, pushing ourselves to the limit and still feeling like we've fallen short. The result? Burnout, missed opportunities, and relationships—whether with a partner or ourselves—taking a backseat.

At the end of the day, balance isn't about perfection. It's about recognizing that when one area of life is out of sync, it can affect everything else. Prioritizing connection, self-care, and mindfulness isn't selfish—it's the key to a healthier, happier future.

To avoid exhaustion from overwork, it is essential to take breaks at predetermined times throughout the day.

METHOD TO MADNESS

- Spend time with those that encourage and believe in you.
- Turn off electronics during critical periods.
- Keep your focus on the current moment and let the rest of the day take care of itself.
- Determine what is most important and prioritize it.
- Never be afraid to say NO!
- Set your course and stick to it.
- Focus on what must be addressed.
- Consider your objectives and values.
- Concentrate on the positive aspects of your life and build a grateful mindset.
- Schedule time in your calendar for both work and play.

DESCRIBE SOME OF THE EXCESSES YOU'VE NOTICED AND YOUR PLANS TO REIN THEM IN.

EXCESS	BALANCE

MEDITATION!

Quote:

"To thine own self be true" - William Shakespeare

Meditation has the potential to offer you a sense of calm, peace, and balance, all of which can improve not just your physical health but also your mental and emotional well-being. You can also use it to relax and unwind by focusing your attention on something soothing, which will allow you to relieve stress. Meditation may teach you how to begin each day with an attitude of gratitude and inner calmness, and it can help you learn to do this more effectively. You should be thankful for anything and everything that helps you live a healthy and prosperous life. As everything in this world is interrelated and relevant to one another, the key to achieving success here is to become one with the universe.

It is suggested that you sit quietly in meditation for at least ten minutes each day, you will be astounded by how much more you can take in, absorb, and utilize once you have acquired the skill of appreciating isolation. Since everyone reacts differently to meditation, if meditating for 10 minutes doesn't seem to be having the desired effect, you should try meditating for a longer time.

When meditating your main objectives should be:
- BREATHWORK
- SELF REFLECTION
- POSITIVE VIBRATIONS
- GRATITUDE
- INSPIRATIONS

As we get older, we experience a slow but steady decline in our capacity to maintain concentration over protracted periods. There is simply too much going on for us to be able to focus our full attention on any one particular topic. When we have to concentrate hard on something that requires a lot of mental effort, like reading a book or staring at a screen, we have a natural preference for being alone. Constant routines, long hours spent working and online, as well as a severe lack of sleep. Because your mind is so preoccupied with attempting to relax after absorbing so much information, it is not hard to find things that will distract you.

EXERCISES REQUIRING MEDITATION:

- Pondering
- Dissecting
- Memorising
- Connecting
- Concentrating
- Engaging
- Reading
- Assessing

CHAKRA

In yoga and meditation, the focus is directed at the seven energy centers known as chakras. The spine is said to be in alignment thanks to the seven major chakras that run from the base of the spine to the top of the head. The third eye chakra sits in the middle of the forehead, between the eyes. It has to do with the mystical, the enlightened, and the intuitive. The sixth of the seven chakras that control the human physical, mental, and spiritual bodies is the third eye. It may lead us to a place of enlightenment and expanded awareness. If a person is unable to meditate, an emotional imbalance, such as emotions of insecurity, loneliness, or greed, or a physical imbalance, such as headaches and migraines, digestive issues, or intestinal disorders, may emerge.

DO YOU PARTICIPATE IN MEDITATION?　　　YES OR NO

DO YOU UNDERSTAND CHAKRA?　　　YES OR NO

DO YOU ENGAGE IN CHAKRA OR OTHER FORMS
OF SPIRITUAL MEDITATION?　　　YES OR NO

HAS MEDITATION BEEN BENEFICIAL TO YOU
THROUGHOUT YOUR LIFE?　　　YES OR NO

Topics to Focus on During Meditation:

☐ ____

☐ ____

☐ ____

☐ ____

☐ ____

☐ ____

LISTEN TO THE VOICES!

Quote:

"Follow your instincts. That's where true wisdom manifests itself."
— Oprah Winfrey

If you pay attention to the voice in your head that firmly guides you on different points of view, you are not insane for doing so. Everyone possesses the ability to use their intuition, but not everyone makes the conscious decision to do so. How our unconscious mind conveys information to our conscious mind is through the medium of intuition. It can be challenging to have faith in our abilities and choices at times because it can be tough to identify if we are hallucinating or if what we are feeling is real. However, there are several examples of people who listened to their gut instincts and made wise choices when their futures were on the line.

Even though we might not be aware of it, our thoughts are being recorded, analyzed, and filed away in ways that supply us with the wisdom that is helpful to us. While it is essential to pay attention to your gut feelings, we also require faith and courage to do so. The ability to put your inner strengths to the test and learn how to make the most use of them is one of the most important reasons why training is so important.

We are always aware of whether something is wonderful, terrible, or requires our immediate attention, even if no one else is aware of these things. Some people believe that this is a message from a higher power or your subconscious trying to get your attention and warn you to be careful.

MOMMA KNOWS

Some of us have heard our mothers and grandmothers recount harrowing accounts of things that happened to them in their dreams or visions. Only those who have been allowed to be cared for by their biological mothers or other loving mother figures at some time in their life can genuinely testify to the transforming power of a mother's love. She is the only one who knows all there is to know about her child, and no one can equal her level of knowledge and awareness.

Women have a natural tendency to trust their instincts, which is one of the numerous reasons why they have so many advantages over men in terms of emotions and mental strength. There are several scenarios in which the maternal instinct may be extremely advantageous to her and her offspring, keeping them secure for millennia. These instincts are even present in the animal kingdom and it is always heartwarming to watch.

DREAMS

There's no denying that our lucid dreams are part of a larger network. Dreams can surprise us even if we have some idea of what we expect them to be about.

Some people think that our souls can't rest while our bodies sleep and that we only really "live" when we're asleep. Could this be the mysterious fourth dimension, being revealed? Is it possible that we can catch a glimpse of the afterlife in our dreams? There are many views on the phenomenon of sleep and dreaming and the beauty of life is that we won't know until we are dead.

I occasionally wonder if the individuals I care about, or even those I don't, have the same pattern of recurring, inexplicable dreams as I do. It's normal to be intrigued by repeated dreams, especially if they include people you don't believe belong in your dream world. Not to mention nightmares.

Whether or not they can connect to your dreams, most of us feel embarrassed or ashamed to discuss them. Though our imaginations might get away with us at times, it's still perfectly lawful to talk about them.
When you wake up from a dream, you normally forget a lot of the specifics, proving that not everything in a dream is designed to be remembered.

Keeping a dream journal is one technique to investigate the significance of one's dreams. It may surprise you with knowledge about your present position.

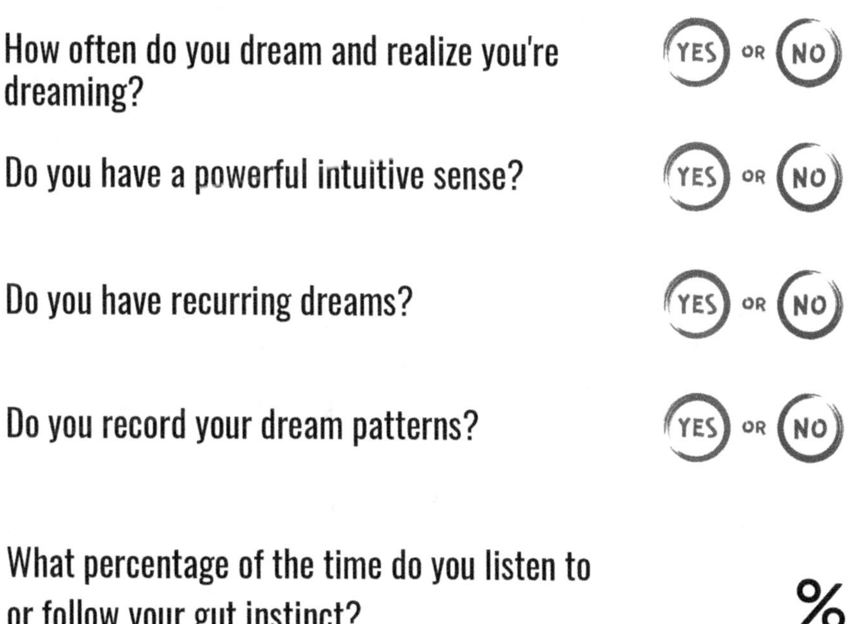

Recall a memorable dream or significant vision:

What are your thoughts on life after death?

COLOR ME AURA!

Quote:

"Energy is contagious, positive and negative alike. I will forever be mindful of what and whom I am allowing into my space." - Alex Elle.

Other people will continue to see the AURA regardless of whether or not you believe in it, and they will base their decisions on what they sense.

AURA | ENERGY | VIBE

You won't be able to see or touch it, but you will be able to sense its presence. It seems as if a halo of ethereal energy were around your body at this very moment. The vast majority of individuals think that they can pick up on another person's "Vibe;" yet there are others who either do not believe this or are unable to identify what it is. Although there isn't a huge amount of difference between the two, different countries and cultures call these events by a variety of names.

When you engage in conversation with another person, you are allowed to evaluate not just their individual qualities but also their demeanor in general. The color of a person's aura can provide information not only about that person's personality but also about the personalities of those who are in their immediate vicinity. Because auric fields are present in and around all living things, it is essential to have a solid understanding of them.

If the color of your aura shifts, it may be an indication that you are sick, and having a healthy aura is a good sign of your overall state of health.

By taking a snapshot of someone's aura before any noticeable symptoms appear, it's possible to determine if they're unwell. A person's emotional condition can be sensed, and they may gain insight into their life's purpose. Each individual has a unique energy, with some feeling a sense of familiarity or isolation. It's common to experience hallucinations or visual disturbances if your thoughts, perceptions, or level of awareness change.

If you want to sense someone's aura, it's important to avoid overwhelming your mind with too many details. Instead, maintain a clear focus on your surroundings and keep your eyes relaxed. Keep in mind that human eyesight is not a straight line, so even if you're looking directly at someone's nose, your peripheral vision can help you observe the sides of their face.

SHOULD YOU CARE ABOUT YOUR AURA?

Your aura is like your energy signature—it changes based on what's happening in your life. Had a bad day? Your aura might feel heavy. Had a killer workout and feel amazing? It's probably bright and popping. It's basically a reflection of what's going on inside, which makes it kinda cool to think about.

Some people say they can see auras around others, like colorful light outlines. But for most of us, it's more about vibes. You know when you meet someone and instantly feel good—or maybe you get weird, bad vibes for no reason? That's their aura affecting you. You don't have to see it to feel it.

THE SCIENCE VS. SPIRITUALITY DEBATE

Okay, so science isn't exactly on board with the whole "energy field" thing. But whether or not it's real, the idea of an aura is a cool way to think about how you affect the world around you. It's like a reminder to take care of yourself so your energy (and your vibe) is on point.

WHY IT'S A VIBE

Auras are more than just mystical fluff—they're a way to think about how your mood, emotions, and energy impact the world. Whether you're manifesting your dream life, journaling about your growth, or just vibing, your aura reflects your inner glow. Keep it bright, and remember: your vibe attracts your tribe.

LEVELING UP YOUR AURA

Want to keep your vibe strong?

Meditate: Chill out and clear your mind. Good vibes only.

Stay Grounded: Spend time in nature or just unplug for a while. Your aura loves fresh air and good energy.

Protect Your Energy: Imagine a bubble of light around you when dealing with negative people. It's like turning on "Do Not Disturb" for your aura.

Notes:

AURA

Think of an aura as your personal energy vibe. It's like an invisible glow around you that reflects your mood, personality, and even how you're feeling physically or mentally. Some people believe they can see these vibes as colors, while others just "sense" them, kind of like picking up on someone's mood the second they walk into a room.

Here's the fun part: every aura has colors, and each color supposedly says something about your vibe. Think of it like a personal Spotify Wrapped, but for your energy:

SILVER
A silver aura reflects intuition, creativity, and spiritual growth, often linked to abundance and wisdom.

ORANGE
A sign of self-assurance, excitement, and a person who takes charge in relationships.

GREEN
A healing, earthy vibe. You're probably the person your friends vent to because you just get it.

MAGENTA
This aura colour take their creative drive and utilise it in every aspect of their lives. Their main goal is always to be unique and brave.

PURPLE
Deep, spiritual, and a little mysterious. You love people no matter what, and desire spiritual love.

PINK
A person who is a giver in relationships and is often taken for granted.

RED
You're passionate, fiery, or maybe just straight-up stressed. Big "main character energy," but also "don't mess with me" vibes.

YELLOW
Creative, bubbly, and full of ideas. The kind of energy that screams "sunshine emoji."

INDIGO

An Indigo Aura are often very intuitive, which means they can understand things without needing to be told. Honest and direct in relationships.

TURQUOISE

A habit of moving from one relationship to the next.

BROWN

Someone who is totally focused on themselves and their needs, to the detriment of everyone else.

BLUE

Emotionally sensitive and are self-expressive. For the most part, they're are well-trusted and deeply value honesty and sincerity.

BLACK

This aura can reveal people who struggle with suppressed negative emotions or an energy blockage, like an unbalanced.

WHITE

Displays an intellectual and emotional willingness to learn and grow.

Connect the Aura color to what it represents:

GROWTH	PURLE
POWERFUL	ORANGE
LOVE	BLUE
CREATIVITY	PINK
RAREST	GREEN
INTUITION	RED
SADNESS	WHITE

The colors of your aura can reveal the type of energy you are currently receiving, giving off, and sharing with those around you. Remember that our energies are always changing and moving. It's possible you may see a change in the colors and placement of your aura within a few months.

USING COLORED PENCILS, FILL IN AND SUMMARIZE YOUR AURA OVER THE NEXT 12 MONTHS. NOTE CHANGES AND WHY.

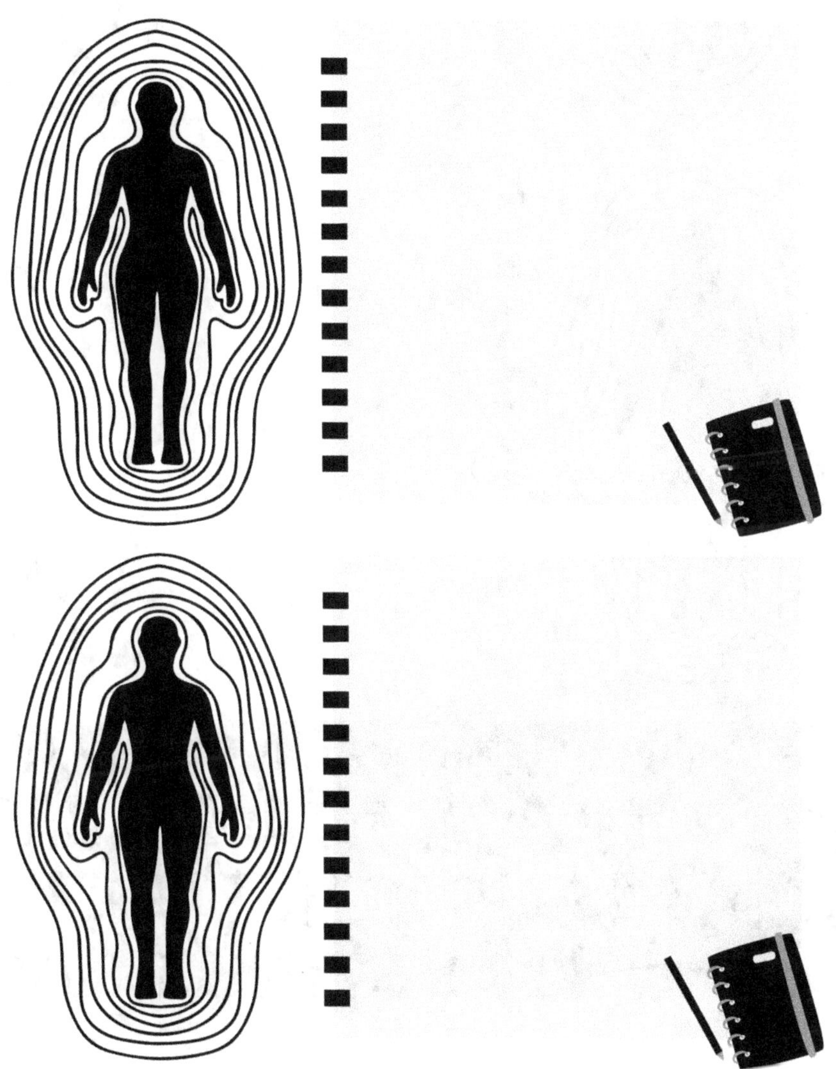

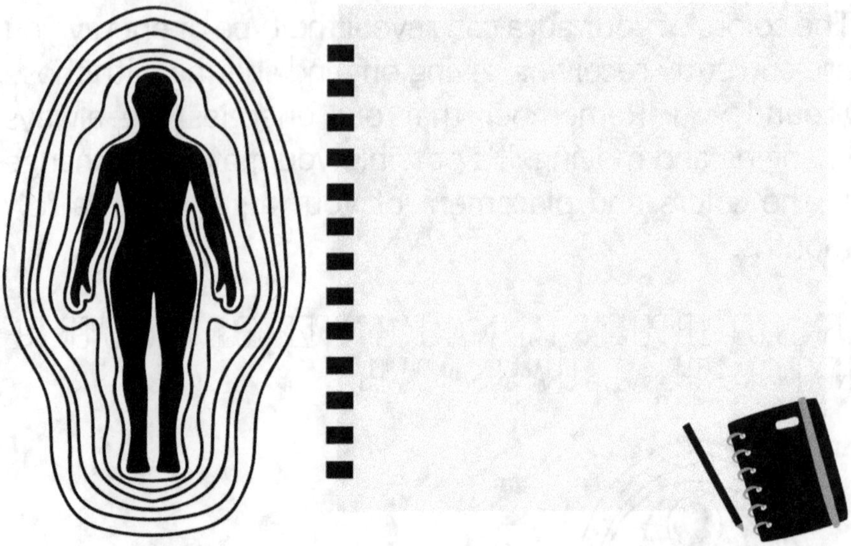

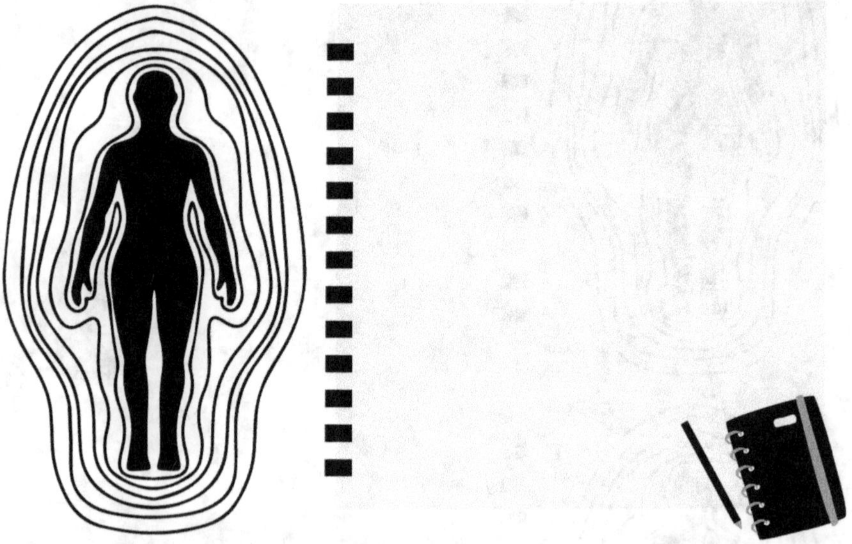

Instead of leaving a large sum of money, it may be more meaningful to leave books and letters that reflect your true nature for your loved ones. These items can endure for a longer period of time.

Soul Notes

25 GEMS

 RELATIVES ARE BLOODLINES; FAMILY IS LOVE, DEDICATION, AND CARE. DON'T FEEL BAD ABOUT LEAVING TOXIC RELATIVES.

 IF HE CHEATED WITH YOU OR ON YOU, THERE'S A GOOD CHANCE THAT HE WILL DO IT AGAIN, EVEN IF IT'S YEARS FROM NOW.

 WHAT ARE YOU WORKING TOWARD IF YOU DON'T HAVE A PLAN? WHAT ARE YOUR PLANS, HOPES, AND DREAMS? IF YOU DON'T HAVE ANY, YOU JUST LIVE DAY TO DAY.

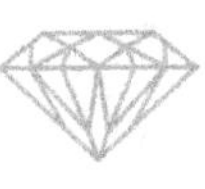 THERE WILL ALWAYS BE SOMEONE WHO IS BETTER LOOKING, SMARTER, FUNNIER, COOKS BETTER, OR HAS MORE MONEY THAN YOU DO. THE QUESTION IS WHY DO YOU LIVE TO MAKE SOMEONE ELSE HAPPY?

 YOUR CHILD OR CHILDREN DIDN'T ASK TO BE HERE! THEY ALSO DIDN'T CHOOSE TO HAVE A HARD, AVERAGE, AND LESS DESIRABLE LIFE THAN OTHER KIDS.

 DON'T ASSUME THAT EVERYONE ON THE ROAD CAN DRIVE OR HAS A LICENSE. BE VIGILANT AND DILIGENT!

 AVOID THOSE WHO MAKE AN ATTEMPT TO MAKE YOU LOOK SMALL OR WHO OPENLY HUMILIATE YOU. THEY ARE NOT YOUR PEOPLE.

 USE ELECTRONIC DEVICES FOR GOOD. RESPECT YOUR PRIVACY AND THE PRIVACY OF OTHERS.

 NEVER MAKE DECISIONS ON IMPULSE. TAKE TIME TO CONSIDER ALL ASPECTS OF THE SITUATION.

 ADDRESS YOUR EMOTIONS ON THE SAME DAY; NEVER LET YOUR EMOTIONS AND UNSOLVED CONCERNS LINGER INTO THE NEXT DAY.

 BE ORIGINAL. BE UNIQUE. THE WORLD IS WATCHING!

 NEVER FORCE SOMEONE TO WALK DOWN THE AISLE. IF YOU ARE SUCCESSFUL, YOU MAY FIND YOURSELF IN A MARRIAGE BY YOURSELF.

 NO RELATIONSHIP IS WORTH THE RISK TO YOUR EMOTIONAL AND PHYSICAL WELLBEING.

 WALK AWAY AND LIVE TO SEE ANOTHER DAY.

 IT IS IMPOSSIBLE TO ALTER SOMEONE WHO REFUSES TO CHANGE. THIS IS AN INTERNAL PROBLEM WITH AN INTERNAL SOLUTION.

 PRIORITIZE QUALITY BEFORE QUANTITY!

 MAKE IT A GOAL TO SPEND YOUR LIFE WITH AS FEW REGRETS AS YOU POSSIBLY CAN.

 THOSE WHO ARE HURT HURT OTHER PEOPLE, WHO THEN GO ON TO HURT MORE PEOPLE!

 WE DON'T GET TO CHOOSE OUR RELATIVES, BUT WE CAN CHOOSE OUR FRIENDS AND FAMILY!

 NEVER LOVE A MAN MORE THAN HE LOVES YOU!

 IT'S NEVER A GOOD IDEA TO GET MARRIED BECAUSE OF AN UNPLANNED PREGNANCY.

 NO RELATIONSHIP IS WORTH THE RISK TO YOUR EMOTIONAL AND PHYSICAL WELLBEING.

 PEOPLE KNOW MORE THAN YOU THINK!

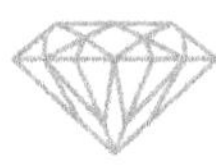 NOT EVERYTHING THAT SHINES IS ACTUALLY VALUABLE.

 YOU'RE BRAVER, STRONGER, SMARTER, AND LOVED MORE THAN YOU REALIZE!

Thank you for your purchase of *'1 Thing Momma Didn't Tell Us.'* I hope you found it insightful.

If you enjoyed the book, I would greatly appreciate it if you would consider sharing it with your family and friends, and perhaps leaving an online review. Your feedback and support are invaluable and motivate me to continue creating work I'm passionate about.

Find us on 

For Information and Inquiries: boss.mentality2020@gmail.com
BOSS MENTALITY INC. PRODUCTIONS

HOOP DREAMS: D1 Basketball • Athlete's Personal Planner & Guide

By: K. J'heneil • 8.5x11

Regardless of one's high school year, this book will provide the necessary information to become a college basketball recruit and prepare for a top-level playing future. Players and their families can use this vital information to plot a practical path to collegiate basketball and avoid spending resources on fruitless pursuits.

Learn to build your athletic presence, create a training and development schedule, find a coach, establish a diet, track academic grades, and a lot more.

Purchasing this customized planner and companion guide will undoubtedly rank highly among the most wise investments along the way, as you make your HOOP DREAMS a reality.